OSCAR WILDE

MODERN LITERATURE SERIES

GENERAL EDITOR: Philip Winsor

In the same series:

(*continued on last page of book*)

OSCAR WILDE

Robert Keith Miller

FREDERICK UNGAR PUBLISHING CO.

NEW YORK

Copyright © 1982 by Frederick Ungar Publishing Co., Inc.
Printed in the United States of America

Library of Congress Cataloging in Publication Data

Miller, Robert Keith, 1949-
  Oscar Wilde.

  (Modern literature series)
  Bibliography p.
  Includes index.
  1. Wilde, Oscar, 1854-1900.   2. Authors,
Irish—19th century—Biography.   I. Title.
II. Series.
PR5823.M5   1982   828'.809 [B]   81-70734
ISBN 0-8044-2629-5   AACR2

Contents

Chronology

1854   OCTOBER 16 Oscar Wilde is born in Dublin, the second son of Dr. William Wilde and Jane Francesca Wilde.

1864   Dr. Wilde is knighted by Queen Victoria in recognition for his services to "Statistical Science, especially in connection with the Irish Census."

1864–71   Oscar Wilde attends Portora Royal School, Enniskillen, Ireland.

1871–74   Oscar Wilde attends Trinity College, Dublin.

1874   FEBRUARY Wilde wins the Berkeley Gold Medal for Greek.

        OCTOBER Wilde begins his studies at Magdalen College, Oxford.

1875   JUNE With John Mahaffy, Professor of Ancient History at Trinity, Wilde tours Italy.

1876   APRIL 19 Sir William Wilde dies.

1877   MARCH–APRIL Wilde visits Greece with Mahaffy, returning by way of Rome.

1878   JUNE 10 Wilde wins the Newdigate Prize for his poem, *Ravenna*.

        NOVEMBER 28 Wilde receives his B.A. degree.

1879   Wilde settles in London.

1881   JUNE *Poems*, Wilde's first book, is published in London.

DECEMBER 24   Oscar Wilde sails for New York.

1882   For the entire year, Wilde lectures in America.

1883   WINTER   Wilde lives in Paris, where he writes *Vera* and *The Duchess of Padua*, his first two plays.

MAY   Returning to London, Wilde takes rooms at 9 Charles Street, Grosvenor Square.

AUGUST   In order to supervise the first production of *Vera*, Wilde visits New York. The play is a failure, and he returns to London in September.

SEPTEMBER 24   Wilde begins a lecture tour of the United Kingdom.

NOVEMBER 26   In Dublin, Wilde becomes engaged to Constance Lloyd.

1884   MAY 29   Oscar and Constance Lloyd are married in St. James Church, Sussex Gardens, London.

MAY–JUNE   Mr. and Mrs. Oscar Wilde honeymoon in Paris and Dieppe.

1885   JANUARY 1   The Wildes move into their carefully redecorated home, 16 Tite Street, Chelsea.

JUNE 5   Wilde's first child is born—a son, Cyril.

1886   Wilde meets Robert Ross, a young Canadian, with whom he would become close friends.

NOVEMBER 3   Wilde's second son, Vyvyan, is born.

1887   APRIL   Wilde becomes editor of *The Woman's World*.

1888   MAY   *The Happy Prince and Other Tales* is published by David Nutt.

1889   JULY   Wilde gives up the editorship of *The Woman's World*.

1890   JUNE 20   *The Picture of Dorian Gray* is published in *Lippincott's Monthly Magazine*, Philadelphia.

1891   FEBRUARY   "The Soul of Man Under Socialism"
            is published in *The Fortnightly Review*.

            MAY   *Intentions* is published by Osgood,
            McIlvaine & Co.

            JULY   *The Picture of Dorian Gray* is pub-
            lished in book form by Ward, Lock, & Co.

            *Lord Arthur Savile's Crime and Other
            Stories* is published by Osgood, McIlvaine & Co.

            Wilde meets Lord Alfred Douglas.

            NOVEMBER   *A House of Pomegranates* is
            published by Osgood, McIlvaine & Co.

            NOVEMBER–DECEMBER   Wilde writes *Sa-
            lomé* in Paris

1892   FEBRUARY 20   *Lady Windermere's Fan* opens
            in London.

            JUNE   *Salomé* is banned by the Lord
            Chamberlain.

            AUGUST–SEPTEMBER   Wilde writes *A
            Woman of No Importance*.

1893   FEBRUARY 22   *Salomé* is published in French
            by the Librairie de l'Art Indépendant, Paris.

            APRIL 19   *A Woman of No Importance* is
            produced.

            JUNE–OCTOBER   Wilde lives with Lord
            Alfred Douglas at The Cottage, Goring-on-
            Thames.

            OCTOBER   Wilde takes rooms at 10 and 11
            St. James Place, where he writes *An Ideal Hus-
            band*.

            NOVEMBER 9   *Lady Windermere's Fan* is
            published by Elkin Mathews and John Lane "at
            the Sign of the Bodley Head."

1894   FEBRUARY 9   *Salomé* is published in English by
            John Lane with illustrations by Aubrey
            Beardsley.

            MAY   Wilde goes to Florence with Lord
            Alfred Douglas.

            JUNE 11   *The Sphinx*, a poem by Oscar

Wilde, is published by Elkin Mathews and John Lane.

AUGUST–SEPTEMBER   Wilde   lives   at Worthing, where he writes *The Importance of Being Earnest*.

OCTOBER 9   *A Woman of No Importance* is published by John Lane.

1895   JANUARY 3   *An Ideal Husband* opens in London.

JANUARY–FEBRUARY   Wilde visits Algiers with Lord Alfred Douglas.

FEBRUARY 14   *The Importance of Being Earnest* opens in London.

FEBRUARY 28   Wilde finds, at his club, a card from the Marquess of Queensberry: "To Oscar Wilde, posing as a sodomite."

MARCH 1   Wilde obtains a warrant for the arrest of Queensberry.

MARCH   With Lord Alfred Douglas, Wilde visits Monte Carlo.

APRIL 3   The Queensberry libel trial begins.

APRIL 5   The Marquess of Queensberry is acquitted; Oscar Wilde is arrested for "committing indecent acts."

APRIL 6–26   Oscar Wilde is imprisoned at Holloway Gaol.

APRIL 26   Oscar Wilde is tried at the Old Bailey.

MAY 1   The jury disagrees, and a new trial is ordered.

MAY 7   Wilde is released on bail.

MAY 20   Wilde's second trial begins.

MAY 25   Oscar Wilde is sentenced to two years in prison with hard labour, the maximum penalty allowed by law. He is sent to Pentonville Prison.

JULY 4   Wilde is transferred to Wandsworth Prison.

NOVEMBER 12   Wilde is examined in Bankruptcy Court.

	NOVEMBER 20 Wilde is transferred to Reading Gaol.
1896	FEBRUARY 3 Lady Wilde dies in London.
	FEBRUARY 11 *Salomé* is produced in Paris.
1897	JANUARY–MARCH Wilde writes *De Profundis*.
	MAY 19 Released from prison, Wilde leaves for France the same day, never to return to England.
	MAY 26 Wilde settles in a small village near Dieppe, Berneval-sur-Mer.
	MAY–OCTOBER Wilde writes *The Ballad of Reading Gaol*.
	SEPTEMBER 4 Wilde is reunited with Lord Alfred Douglas at Rouen.
	SEPTEMBER–NOVEMBER Wilde lives with Douglas in Naples.
1898	FEBRUARY 13 *The Ballad of Reading Gaol* is published by Leonard Smithers.
	MARCH Wilde moves to the Hotel d'Alsace, Paris. It would be his home for the better part of the next two years.
1899	FEBRUARY *The Importance of Being Earnest* is published by Leonard Smithers.
	JULY *An Ideal Husband* is published by Leonard Smithers.
1900	APRIL–MAY Wilde travels in Italy and Sicily, making a side trip to Switzerland on his way back to Paris.
	OCTOBER 10 Wilde undergoes an operation on his middle ear to correct damage that had resulted from an accident in prison.
	MID-NOVEMBER An abscess develops in the ear that had been operated on; doctors diagnose cerebral meningitis.
	NOVEMBER 30 Oscar Wilde dies in his room at the Hotel d'Alsace.
	DECEMBER 3 Wilde is buried at Bagneux Cemetery.
1902	NOVEMBER · Max Reinhardt produces *Salomé* in Berlin.

1905   FEBRUARY   Heavily edited by Robert Ross, *De Profundis* is published in Germany by S. Fischer (translation by Max Meyerfield). Its success prompts Methuen & Co. to offer an edition in English.

DECEMBER   Richard Strauss produces his operatic version of *Salomé* at Dresden. The Wilde estate becomes solvent.

1908   Methuen & Co. publishes the first collected edition of Wilde's work—thirteen volumes, edited by Robert Ross.

1909   JULY 19   Wilde's remains are removed from Bagneux to their present resting place at Père Lachaise.

1

Feasting with Panthers: The Rise and Fall of Oscar Wilde

Eccentricity seems to have come to Oscar Wilde as a birthright. His parents, Sir William and Lady Wilde, were both extraordinary; intelligent and accomplished, they were distinctly odd characters within the confines of their Victorian world.

The author of twenty books, ranging from what was for many years the standard textbook on aural surgery to numerous volumes on Irish history, Sir William Wilde was a successful eye and ear surgeon in Dublin. His reputation was international. The Emperor Maximilian visited him en route to Mexico; Napoleon III sent a commissioner from France to consult with him, and the King of Sweden decorated him with the Order of the Polar Star. Appointed Surgeon Oculist in Ordinary to Queen Victoria, he was knighted in reward for extensive contributions to the Irish Census.

On the surface, it would seem that Sir William Wilde was an eminent Victorian. But he had his peculiarities. For one thing, his personal appearance was notorious. George Bernard Shaw remembered him as being "Beyond Soap and Water, as his Nietzchean son was beyond Good and Evil,"[1] and a popular riddle in Dublin society ran: "Why are Sir William Wilde's nails black?" The answer was, "Because he scratches himself."

Addicted to alcohol and renowned for losing his temper, Sir William Wilde was also a well known philanderer, reputed to have a family in every farmhouse. And a sexual scandal ultimately ruined his career. Mary Travers, the daughter of a professor at Trinity College, accused him in 1864 of having chloroformed her some ten years earlier and "violated her person," in the language of the day. The truth was that there was no chloroform involved; Mary Travers was Sir William's mistress. When she realized that he had grown tired of her, she published a pamphlet, which she attributed to Lady Wilde, attacking him for seducing patients in his office. Recognizing that Mary Travers was no simple victim, a jury awarded her damages of only one farthing (about one quarter of one cent) when the case came to court. But Sir William Wilde's reputation was never the same.

Lady Wilde defended her husband stoutly during the Travers trial. Far from being the sort of Victorian lady who would blush at the mention of sex, she saw herself as an artist and a revolutionary and, as such, unfettered by social norms.

Born Jane Francesca Elgee, Lady Wilde was of Italian descent, although her family had been in Ireland since the eighteenth century. She liked to believe that Elgee was a corruption of Alighieri, and that Dante was among her ancestors. This claim was never substantiated, but there was at least one writer within her family: Her grand-uncle was Charles Maturin, author of the popular Gothic novel *Melmoth the Wanderer*.

A fervent Irish nationalist, Jane Elgee adopted the name Speranza, under which she wrote inflammatory articles demanding the independence of Ireland from Britain. The great Potato Famine made the plight of Ireland especially desperate in the 1840s, and in 1848, when revolution seemed to sweep across Europe, Speranza called for "a hundred thousand muskets glittering brightly in the light of heaven . . . circling round the doomed Castle, where the foreign tyrant has held his council of treason and iniquity against our people and our country . . . and then a rising; a rush, a charge from north, south, east and west upon the English garrison, and the land is ours." The British promptly arrested the leaders of the Young Ireland Movement, in whose newspaper this article had appeared. Speranza was not arrested, but when passages from her work were read in court as evidence of treason, she called out from the gallery: "I alone am the culprit. I wrote the offending articles."

No action was ever taken against her, however, and when she married William Wilde three years later, she seems to have put politics aside. As a doctor's wife, and later as Lady Wilde, she channeled her energies into collecting Irish folklore and establishing a literary salon.

Two sons were born to these parents—Willie in 1852, and, in 1854, Oscar Fingal O'Flaherie Wills Wilde. Oscar—named in honor of his godfather, King Oscar I of Sweden—would eventually drop his three middle names, arguing "A name that is destined to be in everybody's mouth must not be too long."

Sir William and Lady Wilde did not banish their children to the care of a governess, as was common for their class in their time. Even as young children, the two boys were allowed to sit at the dinner table with adults. And as Speranza had put her revolutionary principles sufficiently aside to number among her guests the viceroy and his wife, her sons were exposed at an early age to a world in which intelligent and lively conversation was valued.

When he was eleven, Oscar Wilde entered a prestigious boarding school, the Portora Royal School, which had been founded by Charles II. Wilde later described himself as a "healthy young barbarian" at this stage in his life, who was interested in reading only what pleased him. But this is something of a misrepresentation. In his last year at Portora, Wilde won the school prize for Greek Testament, a gold medal in classics, and an entrance scholarship to Trinity College, all of which suggest a serious capacity for learning.

Although Wilde may have seemed, in later life, to be shallow, his education was thorough and his achievements outstanding. At Trinity, which he entered at sixteen, he made first class in his examinations, won an additional scholarship, the composition prize for Greek verse, and, in his third year, the Berkeley Gold Medal for Greek. He climaxed these achievements by winning, in 1874, a scholarship to Magdalen College, Oxford.

Academically, Wilde's career at Oxford was as distinguished as his career at Trinity; he won, among other awards, the coveted Newdigate Prize for Poetry. And during these years, he came under the influence of two men who would have a lasting effect upon the development of his thought—John Ruskin and Walter Pater.

The celebrated author of *Modern Painters* and *The Stones of Venice*, Ruskin was regarded as a seer by some of the best minds of the nineteenth century. He taught that one can judge a civilization by its art, and he argued that great art was no longer possible in England because it had grown materialistic and unjust. Deeply concerned by the plight of the working class, Ruskin urged his privileged students to experience manual labor for themselves, leading them to build a two-mile road for which Wilde helped to break the stone. It was to Ruskin that Wilde owed the social conscience that would eventually find voice in "The Soul of Man Under Socialism."

Leading him in a different direction was another distinguished professor, Walter Pater, author of *Studies in the History of the Renaissance* and *Marius the Epicurian*. Pater preached the doctrine of "art for art's own sake," and he argued that one's highest duty is to oneself—to live life as deeply and completely as possible by "forever curiously testing new opinions and courting new impressions, never acquiescing in a facile orthodoxy." When he urged men to stir their senses through "strange dyes, strange colours, and curious odours" and above all to burn always with "a hard gemlike flame," he found a sympathetic audience in the young Wilde. Pater's elaborate and carefully wrought prose became for Wilde "the holy writ of beauty." It provided him not only with a stylistic model for his own prose but also with an intellectual justification for the pursuit of sensual pleasure.

Between them, Ruskin and Pater encouraged a revolt against the aesthetic standards of late Victorian England. One result was what is often referred to as the Aesthetic Movement, the avant garde movement of the 1870s. There was no fixed creed holding together the diverse men and women who considered themselves as aesthetes. They were linked only in their common pursuit of beauty and in their revulsion for official taste, which in both literature and the decorative arts they found to be heavy and didactic.

Unorthodox by nature, Wilde associated himself with aestheticism as an undergraduate in the same way in which more recent students have proclaimed their modernity by adopting whatever artistic or political philosophy seems to be the most advanced. He collected blue and white china and created a sensation by dressing extravagantly in knee breeches and silk stockings, worn with a braided velvet coat and a large green tie—a costume that seemed to proclaim: "I am an artist, and not like other men."

Declaring that a reformation in dress was far more important than a reformation in religion—and adding that Luther's neckties must have been deplorable—Wilde brought this costume to London when he left Oxford in 1878. He described himself as an art critic and professor of aesthetics and declared to a friend: "I'll be a poet, a writer, a dramatist. Somehow or other I'll be famous, and if not famous, I'll be notorious."[2]

When Wilde arrived in London, he had behind him a distinguished academic career but few important friends and very little money. Moreover, nothing he had learned at the university was designed to prepare him to earn a living. Within months, however, he managed to turn himself into a celebrity: a poet who had yet to publish any poetry outside of collegiate literary magazines and an art critic simply by virtue of describing himself as such.

Wilde understood that people, for the most part, are inclined to take one at one's own evaluation. If one looks like a genius, and talks like a genius, then it is only a question of time—if one is invited to the right parties—before one comes to be perceived as a genius. Perhaps the most unusual aspect of Wilde's career is the way in which he was able to establish himself as a public figure through force of personality.

Adopting the sunflower and the lily as his trademarks, Wilde courted the public eye at every opportunity, believing that there is no such thing as bad publicity. And as one of his best biographers has observed:

Nothing could draw attention to him so surely as strange flowers and strange clothes, for notoriety can be obtained by what one wears more easily than by what one says or does. In this way he became publicly identified with "the Aesthetic Movement" and was soon regarded as the leader merely because he dressed the part. The other aesthetes were not so fortunate. After all one cannot . . . hang a picture of the modern school around one's neck. But the dress-reformer is his own publicity agent, and to the rage of many artists who were producing good work in other fields Oscar gained the kudos which should have been theirs and got them laughed at into the bargain.[3]

Wilde was also careful to associate himself with other celebrities, especially beautiful women. When the great French actress Sarah Bernhardt made her first appearance in England, she was greeted, as she stepped ashore, by Oscar Wilde—crying "Vive Sarah Bernhardt" and throwing an armful of lilies at her feet. Ingratiating himself in this way, Wilde was soon to be found frequently at Bernhardt's side, acting as her interpreter and advisor. Similarly, he managed to become good friends with Lily Langtry, who was the mistress of the Prince of Wales and considered the most beautiful woman of her generation. She called him her "kind tutor" and frequently sought his advice.

It was only in June 1881, over two years since he had arrived in London, that Wilde published his first book, a collection of poems that are now largely unread. At the time, however, the volume enjoyed a moderate success because Wilde had already managed to get people to think of him as a successful poet through his skillful use of what today would be called public relations.

In April 1881, Gilbert and Sullivan opened *Patience*, a satire of aestheticism, and it was widely assumed that its principle character was modeled on Wilde. Although the evidence suggests that Gilbert and Sullivan had another poet in mind, Wilde made sure to be seen at an early performance and quickly identified himself with the role in question.[4]

Patience was a great success in London, but it was uncertain how it would fare in the United States. Richard D'Oyly Carte, who produced the Gilbert and Sullivan operettas, was preparing to open the show in New York. Fearing that American audiences might not appreciate the satire because they were unfamiliar with the ideas upon which it was based, D'Oyly Carte hired Oscar Wilde to give a series of lectures in America. The idea was to take Wilde—all six foot three of him —dress him up in black velvet, put a lily in his hand, and set him forth to astonish the American public. The entire trip was conceived as a publicity stunt on behalf of Gilbert and Sullivan, and it could have easily made Wilde look ridiculous. But for all his newly acquired recognition, Wilde was still only a minor poet. He was determined to seize upon the opportunity and use it to his own advantage. On Christmas Eve, 1881, Wilde set sail for New York.

Forewarned by the agents of the D'Oyly Carte Opera Company, the New York press corps was on hand to see Wilde come ashore. He did not let them down. Announcing at customs that he had nothing to declare but his own genius, Wilde proved to be such good copy that his name became familiar across the entire continent. What began as a modest series of lectures along the east coast was soon expanded into a six-month tour of the nation in which Wilde established himself as an important figure in his own right. Before he was through, Wilde had spoken not only in such major cities as New York, Philadelphia, Washington, Boston, and Chicago but also in places like Fort Wayne, Indiana and Omaha, Nebraska—unusual territory one hundred years ago for an exotic foreigner speaking on such topics as "The House Beautiful" and "The English Renaissance of Art."

Perhaps the unlikeliest stop on his itinerary was Leadville, Colorado, high in the Rocky Mountains. Reputed to be one of the roughest cities in the world, Leadville was fascinated by the portly poet. Wilde reported:

I read them passages from the autobiography of Benvenuto Cellini and they seemed much delighted. I was reproved by my hearers for not having brought him with me. I explained that he had been dead for some little time which elicited the inquiry, "Who shot him?"

Taken afterwards to a dance hall, Wilde was impressed by the printed notice above the piano:

Please do not Shoot the Pianist
He is Doing His Best[5]

The climax of his visit was a gala supper deep within a mine. Wilde astonished his hosts by the quantity of liquor he could consume. Pronouncing him "a bully boy with no glass eye," the miners presented Wilde with a silver drill after a ceremony in which he had opened a new vein, named "The Oscar" in his honor.

Wilde seems to have genuinely admired America. One might expect this self-consciously elegant advocate of European high culture to have condescended to his American audiences. But one learns that Wilde was no simple snob. For example, he admired the state university at Lincoln, Nebraska, and later explained to the press:

It is better for the country to have a good general standard of education than to have, as we have in England, a few desperately over-educated, and the remainder ignorant. One of the things that delighted me the most in America was that the universities reached a class that we in Oxford have never been able to reach—the sons of the farmers and people of moderate means.[6]

And when a Cincinnati newspaper proclaimed, "If Mr. Wilde will leave the lilies and daffodils and come west to Cincinnati, we undertake to show him how to deprive thirty hogs of their intestines in one minute," Wilde made sure Cincinnati was included in his tour. (There were limits, however, to how far he was willing to go. When the citizens of Griggsville, Kansas, sent a telegram to Wilde asking him to talk about aesthetics, the busy lecturer settled for cabling in return: "Begin by changing the name of your town.")

Presented as a celebrity, Wilde *became* a celebrity. Four thousand people were waiting at the station to welcome him to San Francisco. And all along his route, Wilde was welcomed by the most distinguished Americans of the day. In Boston he breakfasted with Longfellow and dined with Oliver Wendell Holmes. At Newport, he was entertained by the famous Harvard professor, Charles Eliot Norton. When in Philadelphia, he visited Walt Whitman in nearby Camden, New Jersey. (Whitman was delighted and described Wilde as "genuine, honest, and manly . . . his youthful health, enthusiasm and buoyancy are refreshing.") In Washington, he met Lincoln's only surviving son, Robert Lincoln, then secretary of war under President Chester Arthur. And when Wilde lectured in New Orleans, he was invited by the ex-president of the Confederacy, the seventy-four-year-old Jefferson Davis, to stay with him at his home outside the city.

Such attention was very gratifying to Wilde. He welcomed fame, although he retained his sense of humor. Describing the placards that announced his lectures, Wilde wryly remarked:

I am now six feet high . . . printed it is true in those primary colours against which I pass my life protesting, but still it is fame, and anything is better than virtuous obscurity.[7]

Unfortunately, the years to come would reveal to Wilde that "virtuous obscurity" has its charms. At the moment, however, whether he was being toasted at Delmonico's or arguing with Mormons in Salt Lake City, Wilde could hardly have imagined that in little more than ten years, he would be almost universally scorned.

His American success aside, Wilde returned to England a man with neither a home nor a regular income. But he did have the proceeds from his lectures, which enabled him to settle in Paris for three months in early 1883. He quickly established himself in French literary circles, numbering among his acquaintances Victor Hugo, Emile Zola, Paul Verlaine, and André Gide. Among artists, he was friendly with Edgar Degas, Camille Pissarro, and Henri de Toulouse-Lautrec, who would later paint his portrait. Wilde enjoyed himself thoroughly in Paris and wrote two plays during his stay that have since fallen into well deserved obscurity—*Vera* and *The Duchess of Padua*.

When he had used up the money he had earned in America, Wilde returned to London, hoping to get at least one of his plays produced. Determined to be taken seriously, he cut his hair short and abandoned the aesthetic costumes that had won him attention in earlier years. Henceforth, he would present himself as a fashionable man-about-town.

Unable to interest anyone in *The Duchess of Padua*, Wilde arranged an American production of *Vera*, for which he was paid one thousand dollars. Wilde sailed for New York in August 1883 in order to attend the opening of his first work to find its way onto the stage. Although the lead was played by Marie Prescott, a celebrated actress of the time, and although the production was said to feature "the most gorgeous piece of stage setting ever seen in this country," the

critics were not impressed. *The New York Times* pro-
nounced the play "unreal, long-winded, and weari-
some," while *The New York Herald* declared it "long
drawn, dramatic rot, a series of disconnected essays
and sickening rant."[8] *Vera* closed in less than a week,
and the disappointed playwright returned once more
to England.

It was now imperative for Wilde to earn some
money, and he was able to arrange a lecture tour of
Great Britain and Ireland in which he repeated pretty
much the same lectures he had given in America. In
November he lectured in Dublin, and it was there that
he renewed his acquaintance with a beautiful Irish girl
named Constance Lloyd whom he had first met in
London two years earlier.

Many of Wilde's biographers are scornful of Constance Lloyd—or Constance Wilde, as she was destined to be. She seems to have lacked a sense of humor
and, more seriously, the power to understand the extraordinary man who was to be her husband. On the
other hand, she was an exceptionally beautiful woman
and something of an heiress. (From her grandfather
she had inherited capital sufficient to produce an income of £800 a year, a considerable sum in an age
when a maid might be employed for £25 a year.) And
she was not without talent. Fluent in French and Italian and a gifted pianist, she had received and rejected
three offers of marriage since she first met Wilde. She
loved Wilde and wanted to be his wife.

They were married on May 29, 1884, before a
large crowd consisting not only of family and friends
but also of a public curious to catch a glimpse of the
bridal party, all of whom were dressed in various
shades of yellow, the color with which the aesthetes
had come to be identified. They honeymooned in Paris
and, upon their return to London, began to hunt for a
house. They settled upon 16 Tite Street, one of five

identical houses put up in a row by a speculator in
Chelsea.

Wilde wanted this house to justify his reputation
as an aesthete, so the interior was completely redone—
the interior decoration being designed by Wilde's
friend, James Whistler. The result was startling and
must have seemed both original and modern by the
standards of 1884, when rooms tended to be dark and
cluttered with bric-a-brac. Special wallpaper was im-
ported from Japan, but most of the walls were painted
white in order to display Wilde's collection of draw-
ings. Furniture was kept to a minimum, in order to
create a sense of spaciousness and emphasize a few
good pieces. And the ceiling in the drawing room was
set with peacock feathers. This would be Wilde's home
for the next eleven years, and he was extremely proud
of it.

For the next two years, Oscar and Constance
Wilde seem to have been happily married. A son,
Cyril, was born in June 1885, and another, Vyvyan, in
November 1886. Wilde loved his children, and his
younger son has left a memorable picture of father
and sons at play:

Most parents in those days were far too solemn and pom-
pous, insisting on a vast amount of usually undeserved
respect. My own father was quite different . . . . He would
go down on all fours on the nursery floor, being in turn a
lion, a wolf, a horse, caring nothing for his usually immacu-
late appearance. And there was nothing half-hearted in his
methods of play. One day he arrived with a toy milk-cart
drawn by a horse with real hair on it. All the harness undid
and took off, and the churns with which the cart was filled
could be removed and opened. When my father discovered
this he immediately went downstairs and came back with
a jug of milk with which he proceeded to fill up the
churns. We then tore around the nursery table, slopping
milk all over the place, until the arrival of our nurse put
an end to that game.[9]

For the first three years of his marriage, Wilde was
dependent upon occasional lecture fees and whatever
he could earn by anonymously reviewing books for
newspapers and magazines. But in April 1887, he finally secured a source of regular income. He was asked
to edit a magazine called *The Lady's World*, which
had been launched several months earlier without attracting a significant audience. Wilde accepted the
offer at once, and it is worth noting the changes he
made.

Wilde's object was to convert a journal which had
previously been devoted to "mere millinery" to "the
recognized organ for the expression of women's opinions on all subjects of literature, art, and modern life."
Accordingly he changed the title of the magazine to
The Woman's World, arguing that the old name was
not appropriate to a magazine "that aims at being the
organ of women of intellect." And for his first issue, he
called for an article on "the attitude of the Universities
towards women from the earliest times down to the
present—a subject never fully treated of."[10] In short,
Wilde was prepared to take women seriously—or at
least more seriously than many of his contemporaries
did.

During the two years in which Wilde edited *The
Woman's World*, he contributed a column entitled
"Literary and Other Notes," but he also pursued his
own work, publishing a successful collection of fairy
tales, *The Happy Prince*, in 1888, and his well-known
essay "The Decay of Lying" in January 1889. When
the young William Butler Yeats arrived in London at
this time, Wilde was happy to be of help to him. Later,
Yeats recorded, "I have never and shall never meet
conversation that could match his. . . . I was astonished by this scholar who as a man of the world was so
perfect."[11]

Wilde left *The Woman's World* in July 1889, and

it is from this time onward that we date most of his important work. Within a year he had published *The Picture of Dorian Gray*, a commercial success that he was quick to follow up, publishing, in 1891, *Intentions, Lord Arthur Savile's Crime and Other Stories,* and *A House of Pomegranates* all within a little over six months. Then, between November 1891 and November 1892, he wrote his first three memorable plays: *Salomé, Lady Windermere's Fan,* and *A Woman of No Importance.* It seemed that Wilde's life had become well ordered at last. The respectably married father of two sons, Wilde was, at the age of thirty-five, a successful writer and a welcome guest in the aristocratic society he so much admired. But his career had already neared its peak.

It was during these years that Wilde began to experiment with homosexuality. His first affair can be traced to 1886, when he met a young Canadian named Robert Ross, who would eventually become his literary executor.[12] Ross introduced him to a young man named Alfred Taylor, at whose Bloomsbury home could be met a variety of male prostitutes. To his undoing, Wilde became involved with a number of them, most notably an unemployed valet named Charles Parker who later testified against him at his trial.

Had Wilde confined himself to relationships of this sort, he might have maintained his social position indefinitely, for late-nineteenth-century society was willing, for the most part, to overlook almost any indiscretion so long as it was not made public. But in 1891 Wilde met a young man who would dominate the rest of his life, Lord Alfred Douglas, the twenty-one-year-old son of the eighth Marquess of Queensberry.

Thoroughly spoiled by an indulgent mother and already given over to the love of young boys, Douglas possessed, according to George Bernard Shaw, a "degree of personal beauty that . . . inspires affectionate admiration in men and women indiscriminantely."[13] He was also an aspiring poet, which appealed to Wilde's intellectual interest. And as an aristocrat, he appealed to Wilde's tendency to idealize his social superiors. Here, it seemed, was a perfect companion— rich, beautiful, talented, and gay.

During the first year-and-a-half of their acquaintance, Wilde saw Douglas on only four occasions. But in May 1892, Douglas was forced to leave Oxford, and from this time on, he was with Wilde almost constantly. Wilde was so infatuated with him that he lost all common sense, and Douglas, for his part, enjoyed being courted by a well-known man about town who was fourteen years his senior.

Wilde travelled to Paris with Douglas, and later to Florence and Algiers. Moreover, they began to live together for weeks and sometimes months at a time in a series of houses Wilde rented outside of London. At one such house, the local clergyman came to call and found them both naked in the garden. Wilde claimed to have told the astonished clergyman "you have come just in time to enjoy a perfectly Greek scene," but the clergyman "got very red, gave a gasp and fled from the place"[14] to the amusement of both Wilde and Douglas, who gave no thought to the consequences of such behavior.

When they were separated, Wilde wrote to Douglas regularly, and his letters are the letters of a man possessed. In one letter, which would later be used against him in court, Wilde praised a sonnet Douglas had sent to him in terms that were distinctly compromising: "Your sonnet is quite lovely, and it is a marvel that those red rose-leaf lips of yours should have been made no less for the music of song than for madness of kisses."[15] Ever careless, Douglas put this letter into the pocket of a jacket he later gave away—

it fell into the hands of blackmailers, who eventually brought it to the Marquess of Queensberry.

It is customary to see Wilde's relationship with Douglas as an unqualified disaster. But the truth is more complex. Although Wilde's love for Douglas ultimately led to his imprisonment, and while there exists much evidence to suggest that Lord Alfred Douglas was an extremely unpleasant young man, it cannot be denied that Wilde's greatest triumphs date from the years they spent together. In prison, Wilde would write to Douglas that "during the whole time we were together I never wrote a single line. Whether at Torquay, Goring, London, Florence or elsewhere, my life, as long as you were by my side, was entirely sterile and uncreative."[16] The record suggests otherwise. From February 1893 to February 1895—the two years immediately preceding his arrest, during which his affair with Douglas was at its height—Wilde wrote his two best plays: *An Ideal Husband* and *The Importance of Being Earnest*. Indeed, of all Wilde's major works, only *The Happy Prince* and *The Picture of Dorian Gray* date from before he met Douglas.

In early 1895, Wilde's career reached its peak. With two successes running simultaneously on the London stage, Wilde seemed finally to have vindicated his longstanding claim to genius. Although rumors were by now circulating about his personal habits, he was still a welcome guest in the society he had done so much to amuse. But his personal life was in disarray. On February 28, 1895, the Marquess of Queensberry left a card for Wilde at his club. It read: "To Oscar Wilde, posing as a sodomite."[17]

Encouraged by Douglas, who hated his father and hoped to see him humiliated in court, Wilde sued the Marquess of Queensberry for libel. It was an extraordinary thing to do. For one thing, Queensberry had not openly accused him of sodomy, only of *posing*

as a sodomite—a charge which would be easier to vin-
dicate. Moreover, Wilde had been indiscreet for years.
Carried away by his own sense of dignity and convinced, perhaps, that as a master of language he could
outtalk any charge, Wilde disregarded the advice of
friends who urged him to drop the suit and go abroad
with his wife until the affair blew over. He pressed on,
assuring his attorneys that there were no grounds for
the charge made against him. Queensberry, however,
had money to hire detectives. Wilde's relations with
the young men he had met through Alfred Taylor
were no secret to him. And by suing Queensberry for
libel, Wilde had, in effect, put himself on trial for
homosexuality.

The libel trial opened on April 3, 1895. Representing the Marquess of Queensberry was Edward Carson, an old rival of Wilde's at Trinity College and a
man destined to inflict upon Ireland its present divi-
sion into two separate states. His cross-examination of
Wilde is among the most memorable in British legal
history.[18]

At first, Wilde won the sympathy of the court by
virtue of his wit. Carson read aloud passages from *The
Picture of Dorian Gray*, which he claimed offered
ample proof that Wilde was homosexual, but Wilde
held his own, criticizing Carson for "impertinence and
vulgarity." Carson then went on to read aloud letters
that Wilde had written to Lord Alfred Douglas. Wilde
defended himself by claiming that his letters were
works of art and had not been intended to be taken
literally: "You might as well cross-examine me as to
whether *King Lear* or a sonnet by Shakespeare was
proper."

So long as the questions pertained to literature,
Wilde emerged victorious. But then Carson began a
much more damaging line of questions, examining the
increasingly nervous Wilde about his relations with

the young men he had met through Alfred Taylor. Finally, Wilde made a serious mistake. When asked if he had kissed one particular boy, he replied, "Oh, dear no. He was a peculiarly plain boy. He was, unfortunately, extremely ugly." This enabled Carson to imply that Wilde would have kissed the boy if he were attractive. Demanding to know why Wilde had mentioned that the boy was ugly, Carson threw Wilde into a state of confusion. He began several answers that he could not complete and eventually stammered: "You sting me and insult me and try to unnerve me, and at times one says things flippantly when one ought to speak more seriously." From this moment on, the outcome of the trial was assured. When Carson proposed to call one of the young men in question to the stand, Wilde dropped the case. In an effort to keep further evidence from coming out in order to save Wilde from subsequent prosecution on criminal charges, his attorney, Sir Edward Clarke, conceded that it could be said that Wilde had *posed* as a sodomite. The jury quickly found the Marquess of Queensberry not guilty of libel, and Wilde left the court in disgrace.

But worse was yet to come. Unsatisfied by the damage they had already inflicted upon Wilde, Queensberry's solicitors wrote to the director of public prosecutions the same day, enclosing a transcript of the trial. The decision was then made by the home secretary and future prime minister, Herbert Asquith, to arrest and imprison Wilde. But in order to allow Wilde to flee abroad if he so wished, the warrant for his arrest was temporarily delayed until the last boat-train had left for France. Wilde was urged to leave by most of his friends, but he felt that it would be dishonorable, and he remained in his hotel until the police came to fetch him.

The arrest of Oscar Wilde led to vicious attacks in the press not only against him but against everything with which he was even remotely associated. Public feeling ran so high, for example, that when it was reported that Wilde was reading a yellow book at the time of his arrest, an angry mob formed outside the editorial offices of *The Yellow Book*, a famous periodical of the 1890s, and broke the windows.

There were to be two trials. The first lasted from April 26 to May 1 and ended in a hung jury; the second, which lasted from May 20 to May 25, brought in a verdict of guilty as charged. Telling Wilde that he was guilty of "extensive corruption of the most hideous kind,"[19] the judge sentenced Wilde to two years imprisonment with hard labor, the maximum sentence allowed by law.

However much one might feel that Wilde brought misfortune upon himself through increasingly injudicious behavior, and however little sympathy one may feel for his plight, it is difficult not to believe him the victim of bigotry and hypocrisy. He was refused bail for over a month, for example, on the grounds that "there is no worse crime than that which the prisoners are charged,"[20] in the words of the presiding magistrate, who evidently believed that sexual relations between men, engaged in by mutual consent, are worse than murder, rape, or treason. And it seems incredible, by the standards of our own time, that the court devoted so much time to proving Wilde to be immoral by quoting from his work.

Students who are interested in Wilde would do well to read a full account of his trials, which were peculiar in a number of ways. The transcripts reveal an obsession with the distinctions of social class, for example. The prosecution did not hesitate to name the grooms and coachmen with whom Wilde had been involved, but it took pains to keep other names from public record. When it seemed as if Wilde was about to mention having shared a hotel room with the nephew of the solicitor-general, he was passed a sheet of paper and instructed to write out the name of the man in question but not say it out loud. And it is worth noting that despite a wealth of evidence against him, no charge was ever made against Lord Alfred Douglas, son of one of the most powerful families in England.

Wilde was, by now, a ruined man. He was abandoned by most of the people he had come to think of as his friends, and his income disappeared almost overnight. The sale of his books practically ceased, and *An Ideal Husband* and *The Importance of Being Earnest*, which had been doing a brisk business when the trials began, both closed, even though an attempt was made to prolong the life of the latter by pasting over the author's name on the advertisements. Within a few weeks Wilde was bankrupt, his goods sold at public auction under shocking conditions. As Wilde sat in prison, his beautiful home was invaded by a curious mob who rummaged through his papers, stealing several manuscripts that have yet to reappear. And all his material goods, even his children's toys, were sold at absurdly low prices. An original Whistler, for example, sold for a shilling, about twenty-five cents in purchasing power today.

After his conviction, Wilde was taken to Pentonville Prison, where he was confined for twenty-three hours a day in a badly ventilated cell. Sanitary conditions were extremely primitive, and his bed was made of wooden boards. He found it impossible to sleep or to eat the prison food, which consisted primarily of gruel supplemented with occasional pieces of greasy bacon. Even worse for Wilde was the complete isolation in which he was forced to live. His only contact with his fellow prisoners was the one-hour-a-day exercise period, and he was not allowed to speak to anyone, under penalty of being kept—as he was more

than once—for seventy-two hours in a completely dark
cell. His reading material was initially limited to the
Bible, a prayer book, and a hymn book. He was for-
bidden to keep any personal possessions, not even a
photograph of his wife and children. And he was allowed to write and to receive only one letter every
three months.

In July 1895, Wilde was transferred to Wandsworth Prison, which he found even worse than Pentonville. By this time, he had lost over thirty pounds
and was dangerously close to a complete breakdown.
But Wilde was not completely forgotten. A parliamen-
tary committee had recently denounced the conditions
in British prisons, and one of its members took an
interest in Wilde's case. In November, Wilde was
transferred once again—this time to Reading Gaol,
where he spent the remainder of his prison term and
which he memorialized in a famous poem.

Wilde himself has left a moving account of his
transfer to Reading from Wandsworth:

From two o'clock till half past two on that day I had to
stand on the centre platform at Clapham Junction in convict dress and handcuffed, for the world to look at. I had
been taken out of the hospital ward without a moment's
notice being given to me. Of all possible objects I was the
most grotesque. When people saw me they laughed. Each
train as it came in swelled the audience. Nothing could
exceed their amusement. That was, of course, before they
knew who I was. As soon as they had been informed they
laughed still more. For half an hour I stood in the grey
November rain surrounded by a jeering mob.[21]

One man came up and spat in his face.

Shortly after Wilde's arrival at Reading, his
mother fell seriously ill. A special request was made to
allow Oscar to visit her on what was obviously her
death bed. It was refused, and she died shortly after
learning the news.

But despite the presence of a harsh prison admin-
istrator at Reading, Wilde's condition slowly began to
improve. A few old friends rallied to his support and
petitioned the government to allow him more books.
The prison commissioners agreed, and granted him the
privilege of using paper, pen, and ink. Wilde thereupon began to write the justification for his life that
is popularly known as *De Profundis*.

Restored to reasonably good health, Wilde was
released from prison on May 19, 1897. He left for
France the same day and never returned to England.
Settling in a small village near Dieppe, Berneval-sur-
Mer, Wilde began to write. He sent a long impas-
sioned letter to *The Daily Chronicle* protesting the
treatment of children in prison and another on the
subject of prison reform in general. He then composed
his greatest poem, *The Ballad of Reading Gaol*, completing it by the end of the summer.

During these first few months of freedom, it
seemed possible that Wilde might be reconciled with
his wife. Constance had also settled on the Continent
as a result of the scandal—first in Switzerland and
later in Italy. But the scandal that had ruined her
husband followed her even there. After she was forced
to leave a hotel when the manager discovered who she
was, she changed her name—and the children's name
—to Holland. Nonetheless, she was still deeply concerned for her husband's welfare.

When Lady Wilde died, Constance had traveled
all the way from Genoa so that she could break the
news to her husband in person. And despite the restrictions that had been placed on prison correspondence, they had managed to keep in touch during
Wilde's imprisonment. Now that he was free, Wilde
was anxious to see Constance and especially anxious to
see his children. But Constance asked to be assured
that the affair with Lord Alfred Douglas was over at

last. Wilde would not acknowledge this. He was still captivated by Douglas, and when the two friends were reunited in September, there was no longer any real question of a reconciliation between husband and wife. Within seven months, Constance Wilde was dead.

After his reunion with Lord Alfred Douglas, Wilde ceased to work. Although his friends urged him to restore his reputation by writing more plays, Wilde seems to have been capable of nothing but abandoning himself to the pursuit of the pleasures that had been denied to him in prison. Cut off from the society that had inspired his wit, he began to drink heavily. Chronically short of funds, he fell into the habit of begging money from friends almost daily, even if he happened to be temporarily provided for. He lived briefly in Naples, moved on to Switzerland, and finally made his home in a small hotel in Paris. By the time he had been out of prison for two years, his health had deteriorated badly. Complaining that he was "dying beyond his means," he managed to retain his celebrated wit almost to the end. But there was no fighting cerebral meningitis, probably complicated by syphilis. On November 30, 1900, Oscar Wilde died in Paris. He was only forty-six years old.

2

A Modern Gothic:
The Picture of Dorian Gray

Constructed around a series of highly theatrical scenes and enlivened by remarkably epigrammatic dialogue, *The Picture of Dorian Gray* remains a very readable novel. But it is much more than merely entertaining. Ever since its publication in 1891, many readers have found it to be deeply disturbing. For beneath its glittering surface, *The Picture of Dorian Gray* explores several serious subjects.

This is a story of moral corruption. When we first meet Dorian Gray, he is an attractive young man with all "the passionate purity of youth." He is innocent, if weak, until he looks upon a marvelous portrait that Basil Hallward, a great artist, has painted of him. Like Narcissus, Dorian becomes fascinated by his own beauty, and this prepares the way for his eventual destruction. He offers to sell his soul for eternal youth:

I shall grow old, and horrible, and dreadful. But this picture will remain always young . . . . If it were only the other way! If it were I who was to be always young, and the picture that was to grow old! For that—for that—I would give everything! Yes, there is nothing in the whole world I would not give! I would give my soul for that!

Under the influence of Lord Henry Wotton, a worldly man about town, Dorian throws off all moral restraint and lives a life of passionate self-indulgence. But he has had his wish. He remains physically unchanged, his corruption recorded only upon the picture, which year after year becomes increasingly monstrous. When Dorian murders Basil Hallward, the portrait becomes evidence: "Loathsome red dew" appears on one of the hands "as though the canvas had sweated blood." Although he has always been careful to keep it concealed from public view, Dorian becomes haunted by the fear of the picture being used against him. Finally, he is driven to destroy it. Slashing the canvas with a knife, he destroys what is left of his soul, and thus destroys himself. When his servants enter the room, they find "a splendid portrait of their master as they had last seen him, in all the wonder of exquisite youth and beauty. Lying on the floor was a dead man, in evening dress, with a knife in his heart. He was withered, wrinkled, and loathsome of visage. It was not until they had examined the rings that they recognized who it was."

Although Wilde is often characterized as the vainest of men, it is clear that he recognized that vanity can lead to self-destruction. But *The Picture of Dorian Gray* is no simple moral tract in behalf of modesty. It is ultimately concerned with the nature of self-fulfillment. In particular, it explores the effect of experience upon character, in terms of both direct experience with life and the vicarious experience that is provided by art. In other words, to what extent are we shaped by what we do?

According to Lord Henry Wotton, experience leads to growth of character:

The aim of life is self-development. To realize one's nature perfectly—that is what each of us is here for . . . . People have forgotten the highest of all duties, the duty one owes one's self.

Or:

I believe that if one man were to live out his life fully and completely, were to give form to every feeling, expression to every thought, reality to every dream—I believe that the world would gain such a fresh impulse of joy that we would forget all the maladies of medievalism and return to the Hellenic ideal.

Of course, when Lord Henry calls upon us to forget "the maladies of medievalism," he is asking, in effect, for the rejection of Christianity and the restraints it has imposed. He argues that even sin can be en-nobling:

The body sins once, and it is done with its sin, for action is a mode of purification . . . . The only way to get rid of a temptation is to yield to it . . . . Resist it and your soul grows sick with longing . . .

In short, Lord Henry is an eloquent advocate of the contemporary notion that one should do whatever feels good. He is charming, like all great tempters, but his counsel is corrupting. When Dorian Gray aban-dons himself to the cult of experience, he discovers that vice can be addictive. So far from purging one's soul of longing, experience can stimulate one's appetite to the point at which satisfaction is no longer possible. Although we are told that "one could never pay too high a price for any sensation," it is evident that Dorian is forced to pay a high price indeed. Before long he is in the grip of desires he cannot control. His pursuit of experience leads not to "the Hellenic ideal" but to waterfront opium dens—and ultimately to death at the age of thirty-eight.

It might be argued, however, that Dorian Gray never really discovers experience so much as diversion —he flirts with life rather than engages with it. His goal, as he puts it, is "to become the spectator of one's own life." And eventually this goal becomes more des-perate: "He wanted to escape from himself." Seen in this light, the modern belief in self-development has become grotesque. Whereas experience is traditionally defended as a means of emotional and intellectual growth, with Dorian Gray it becomes the means of dulling the senses and preventing the pain of self-awareness.

It would be a mistake, however, to see *The Picture of Dorian Gray* as necessarily opposed to all forms of experience. Wilde argues not so much against experience as the abuse of experience. An important distinction must be made between experience through which one might learn and grow and experience that serves no purpose beyond sensual gratification. Dorian's misfortune is not that he has lived deeply and well but that he loses the capacity to feel and with it the capacity to merge his life with others'. His life becomes a series of one-night stands, each encounter briefer than the last.

It is perhaps for this reason that Dorian Gray comes to prefer art to life. Although Wilde was very much influenced by the belief that humanity can find meaning in life through art, he was also skeptical of some of the more grandiose conceptions of art that are characteristic of modern culture. "All art is quite useless," he declares in the preface to *Dorian Gray*, and this idea is in sharp contrast to the values of both Basil Hallward and Dorian Gray.

Basil Hallward is an artist of great ambition. He believes that "there is nothing that Art cannot express." So far from settling for decorative effect, he seeks to found a new school, "a school that is to have in it all the passion of the romantic spirit, all the perfection of the spirit that is Greek." At first it seems that Wilde means us to accept this ideal as his own. But it is difficult to do so when we realize that the one painting that fulfills Hallward's conception of art is the picture of Dorian Gray, and it is for this picture that

Dorian sells his soul. In effect, Dorian has sold his soul
for art. Wilde reminds us that art can be valued to
excess.

This reading is borne out by the story of Sibyl
Vane, a great actress only because she has never experienced the reality of human love. When she falls in
love with Dorian Gray, she loses her art. Because he
values art more than love, Dorian then rejects her, and
she dies. In telling this story, Wilde makes it clear that
his sympathies are with Sibyl Vane. She is presented to
us not simply as a clever actress but as a sensitive
young woman who is devoted to her family and unsul-
lied by the tawdry world in which she lives. Even
Basil Hallward, who is appalled at first to think that
Dorian might marry an actress, recognizes Sibyl's virtues when he sees her: "Through the crowd of un-
gainly, shabbily-dressed actors, Sibyl Vane moved like
a creature from a finer world." And when Dorian
begins to criticize her performance, Hallward reminds
him, "Don't talk like that about anyone you love. . . .
Love is a more wonderful thing than Art."

But the real love scene that is about to be played
out at his feet holds less interest for Dorian than the
romantic roles he has seen enacted upon the stage.
Art is presented as an alternative to life; the two cannot coexist. "The moment she touched actual life,"
Lord Henry tells Dorian, "she marred it, and it marred
her, and so she passed away. Mourn for Ophelia, if
you like. Put ashes on your head because Cordelia was
strangled . . . . But don't waste tears over Sibyl Vane.
She was less real than they are." To this shallow counsel, Dorian responds: "You have explained me to
myself, Harry . . . . I felt all that you have said but
somehow I was afraid of it, and I could not express it
to myself. How well you know me!"[1]

Thus begins Dorian's withdrawal from life. He
continues to pursue sexual pleasure, but he never

again looks for love. His relationships become increasingly self-serving, and soon he is happiest only when he is fondling precious gems and fine brocades, for they make no demands upon him. There are moments, however, when even these pleasures become lost to him—they force him into awareness and inhibit the escape from reality that he ultimately finds in drugs.

A careful reading of *The Picture of Dorian Gray* suggests that Wilde had serious reservations about the modern celebration of art. So far from being an advocate of art for its own sake, Wilde showed that our real obligations lie elsewhere. Art, like experience, is good only so long as it contributes to self-development. When it is used as a luxurious means of passing time, it is no better than the drugs to which Dorian eventually falls victim.

By imposing upon the book a properly Victorian conclusion in which vice is roundly condemned, Wilde rejected the sensual self-indulgence with which he is often associated. If we see *Dorian Gray* strictly in terms of its plot, it becomes a proper nineteenth-century tale of what happens to young men who fall victim to temptation. Lose one's virginity, and it is only a question of time before one becomes an habitué of opium dens. The wages of sin are death.

It is impossible, however, not to feel that Wilde was strongly attracted to the temptations he condemned. Most readers are far more likely to remember the novel's lovingly detailed evocation of sensual pleasure than they are to ponder the rather abruptly moralistic conclusion. If *The Picture of Dorian Gray* tries to warn us against sin, the warning is obscured by the tantalizingly lush descriptions of the sins we are supposed to avoid.

It would be more accurate to recognize that *Dorian Gray* is highly ambivalent—the work of a man who was as yet uncertain of his own beliefs. Ultimately, it is best seen as a moral dialogue between conscience and temptation. It is as if two sides of Wilde's own nature are struggling for dominance. And the clearest sign of this is the way in which the principle characters continuously question their own sincerity. As early as the first chapter, we find Basil Hallward telling Lord Henry Wotton:

I believe that you are really a very good husband, but that you are thoroughly ashamed of your own virtues. You are an extraordinary fellow. You never say a moral thing, and you never do a wrong thing. Your cynicism is simply a pose.

When Lord Henry persists in his argument, Hallward tells him: "I don't agree with a single word you have said, and what is more, Harry, I feel sure you don't either."

Hallward may be the most interesting character in the novel. He is in conflict not only with others but also with himself. He is torn between a fear of self-exposure and the public nature of the work he creates. Because he is a great artist, he reveals something of himself in his work. The realization of this makes him unwilling to exhibit his masterpiece, the picture of Dorian Gray, for the portrait reveals what Hallward delicately calls "a curious artistic idolatry"—pretty clearly a euphemism for what is, in effect, his passionate infatuation with a younger man. Although Lord Henry tells him that passion has commercial value— "Nowadays a broken heart will run to many editions" —Basil declares, "I will not bear my soul to shallow prying eyes. My heart shall never be put under their microscope."

If Basil Hallward represents the man who is dedicated to his work and committed to a private vision, Lord Henry Wotton represents the worldly life to which Wilde was fatally attracted. The conflict between hard work on the one hand and aristocratic ease on the other, between the ability to please and the determination to offend, were very real conflicts for Oscar Wilde. And it is the tension between these different values that makes *The Picture of Dorian Gray* so interesting. There is no clear victor within the book any more than there was within Wilde's own life, but the conflict between the moral and the immoral is nonetheless dramatic.

Hallward is important only in the first few chapters of the novel; thereafter he recedes, only to reemerge (for his own murder) in chapters 12 and 13. The Basil Hallward–Lord Henry Wotton conflict then becomes, out of necessity, a conflict between Lord Henry and Dorian Gray. Dorian, the professed voluptuary, is saddled with a role that Basil had filled much more appropriately—he tries to act as Lord Henry's better self, continually urging him to be less cynical. "You cut life to pieces with your epigrams," Dorian declares to Lord Henry, an accusation he frequently repeats as the novel draws to a close: "You would sacrifice anybody, Harry, for the sake of an epigram." And "I can't bear this, Harry! You mock at everything . . . . " These lines really belong to Basil Hallward, but he is dead by this point in the novel, and so they fall to Dorian Gray. It makes no sense, however, for Dorian to be shocked by Lord Henry's cynicism; his sins by now must surely outnumber his patron's. This leads one to suspect that it is not Dorian Gray but Oscar Wilde who is disturbed by the glib immorality that Lord Henry proclaims. Unwilling to allow Lord Henry to speak unopposed, Wilde forces upon Dorian Gray a role that is ridiculously inappropriate.

The conflicts behind *Dorian Gray* become clearer when we realize that no one character speaks for the author. Wilde merges his personality with those of Basil Hallward, Lord Henry Wotton, and even, at times, Dorian Gray. Wilde himself remarked in a letter that "Basil Hallward is what I think I am: Lord Henry what the world thinks of me: Dorian what I would like to be—in other ages, perhaps."[2] The conflicts among these characters are conflicts that Wilde was trying to work out for himself. Ultimately, much of the novel can be seen as what Matthew Arnold called "the dialogue of the mind with itself"—the self-examination characteristic of modern literature.

Bearing this in mind, it is possible to understand the novel's most obvious flaw—the metamorphosis that Dorian Gray undergoes in the last fifty pages of the book. For most of the novel, Dorian has been presented as evil incarnate. When Sibyl Vane kills herself, Dorian successfully hardens himself to avoid the inconvenience of grief. Three years later, when we meet him again, he is the personification of sensuality, responsible, it seems, for corrupting half of London. Finally, when Basil Hallward beseeches Dorian to pray for salvation, the unrepentant sinner rushes at the unwelcome moralist "and dug the knife into the great vein that is behind the ear, crushing the man's head down on the table, and stabbing again and again."

Although Dorian is occasionally troubled by the fear of detection, he is never bothered by anything approaching the nature of guilt. This characterization remains consistent until the end of Chapter 18. James Vane, Sibyl's brother, has vowed to kill the man he holds accountable for his sister's death, and Dorian knows that Vane is finally on his track. Vane is accidently killed, however, and when Dorian views his body, "a cry of joy broke from his lips"—hardly the sort of response one would expect of a sinner on the eve of his conversion. Yet when we turn to the next chapter, we suddenly encounter a new Dorian Gray.

Presumably, the accidental death of his worst enemy
has moved Dorian to the remorse he could not feel
after killing his own best friend. After rebuking Lord
Henry for his cynicism, Dorian proclaims:

> The soul is a terrible reality. It can be bought, and sold,
> and bartered away. It can be poisoned or made perfect.
> There is a soul in each of us. I know it.

This discovery seems to come a little late in the day;
the painting, after all, has been changing for almost
twenty years. But now Dorian is filled with a new
resolve:

> A new life! That is what he wanted . . . . He would never
> again tempt innocence. He would be good.

Unexpected though this resolve may be, it comes
across as sincere; Wilde provides no evidence of hypocrisy. On the contrary, Dorian sounds genuinely
troubled throughout his last conversation with Lord
Henry. But however much Wilde may have wished to
save Dorian Gray, he must have realized that his plot
demanded that Dorian self-destruct. Therefore, the
last chapter of the novel requires an abrupt shift in our
point of view. Only pages after being led to believe
that Dorian might yet manage to redeem himself, we
are asked to see him as a sinner so hardened that he is
compelled to destroy the last shreds of his conscience.
    This shift suggests that Wilde used *Dorian Gray*
not so much to advance a carefully defined set of beliefs but rather to explore conflicts he was unable to
resolve. Although this uncertainty makes the resolution
of the novel psychologically unconvincing, it contributes to the fascination of the work as a whole.

Among the unresolved conflicts of *Dorian Gray*, perhaps none is more striking than the way in which
Wilde treats homosexuality. One of the most daring

aspects of the book is its assumption that men can be in love with one another—hardly a new discovery in 1891, but nonetheless a relatively unexplored subject for English literature. Unfortunately, critics have often been too ready to interpret Wilde's work in light of what we know about his sexuality. And readers should be careful not to focus on this aspect of Wilde to the exclusion of all else. While it is impossible to overlook the implications of homosexuality that run throughout the book, we should view the subject as simply one of the many conflicts with which Wilde was struggling to come to terms.

Lord Henry Wotton's attraction to Dorian Gray is clearly physical; we hear a lot about the youth's "finely-curved scarlet lips," and before long, Lord Henry has filled his house with no less than eighteen pictures of Dorian and presented him with a mirror framed with "white-limbed" ivory cupids. During the early stages of his infatuation, Lord Henry rejoices in his sense of power over the younger man. Being with him was

like playing upon an exquisite violin. He answered to every thrill of the bow . . . . There was nothing that one could not do with him.

If Dorian is unlikely to respond with equal ardor, he is certainly eager to engage in sexual experimentation. How else can one explain his mysterious hold over Alan Campbell? Or Basil Hallward's often-quoted plea:

Why is your friendship so fatal to young men? There was that wretched boy in the Guards who committed suicide. You were his great friend. There was Sir Henry Ashton, who had to leave England, with a tarnished name. You and he were inseparable. What about Adam Singleton, and his dreadful end? What about Lord Kent's only son, and his career? . . . What about the young Duke of Perth? What sort of life has he got now?

Basil Hallward, of all people, should know the answer to the riddle he has posed, for he himself is passionately devoted to Dorian Gray. In a passage that prefigures Wilde's own feelings for Lord Alfred Douglas, Basil tells Lord Henry: "I knew I had come face to face with someone whose mere personality was so fascinating that, if I allowed it to do so, it would absorb my whole nature, my whole soul, my very art itself."

The implications of such passages were not lost on Wilde's audience. (Indeed, passages from *Dorian Gray* were read in court when Wilde was on trial.) Perhaps realizing that he had gone too far, Wilde goes through the motions of providing Dorian with at least one great passion for a woman, the seventeen-year-old Sibyl Vane. But even here there is a distinctly ambivalent note. Dorian proposes marriage to Sibyl Vane only after he has seen her perform as Rosalind in *As You Like It*, a role which demands male impersonation. "You should have seen her!" he declares, "When she came on in her boy's clothes she was perfectly wonderful."

Although Wilde was bold in approaching a subject that was seldom discussed in his time, he nevertheless brings himself to condemn it. All the young men associated with Dorian Gray meet unhappy ends, and Dorian's sexuality is presented as a problem—it leads to his confrontation with Basil Hallward, a confrontation that leads, in turn, to murder.

The question then arises, why did Wilde force his readers to confront the subject at all? Technically, one might argue that it relates to his determination to make Dorian Gray experience everything that life has to offer. But homosexual love is not presented as a matter of casual experimentation. Clearly fascinated by the subject, Wilde constructed the entire novel around a triangle of three men. He used fiction as a means of exploring inner conflicts and forcing people to confront something that was about to become a public issue in his own life. In addition to many other concerns, Wilde used *The Picture of Dorian Gray* as a means of coming to terms with his own sexuality.

There is one additional conflict within this book: it is composed of radically conflicting styles. Half of the book consists of dialogue that remains, for the most part, engaging and original. When Lord Henry Wotton complains that a well known hostess "tried to found a *salon*, and only succeeded in opening a restaurant" or when he declares across a dinner table that "Nowadays people know the price of everything and the value of nothing"[3] the novel prefigures Wilde's emergence as a dramatist in the years to come. Wilde can also be wonderfully clever in giving rapid sketches of his characters. An elderly woman is described as "a perfect saint among women, but so dreadfully dowdy that she reminded one of a badly bound hymn book." And the short paragraph devoted to describing Lady Henry Wotton is marvelously succinct:

She was a curious woman, whose dresses always looked as if they had been designed in a rage and put on in a tempest. She was usually in love with somebody, and as her passion was never returned, she had kept her illusions. She tried to look picturesque, but only succeeded in being untidy. Her name was Victoria, and she had a perfect mania for going to church.

These lines are amusing, and one of the reasons why they are able to amuse is that they are easily digestible. They seem so clever, in fact, that some critics are led to dismiss them as glib. It is this aspect of Wilde that moved Jorge Luis Borges to conclude: "His perfection has been a disadvantage; his work is so harmonious that it may seem inevitable and even trite."[4]

But if we can mine innumerable verbal gems from the pages of *The Picture of Dorian Gray,* we must labor through a good deal of sludge along the way. The novel often seems about to sink beneath the weight of an ornate prose style. The opening paragraphs are a case in point:

> The studio was filled with the rich odor of roses, and when the light summer wind stirred amid the trees of the garden there came through the open door the heavy scent of the lilac, or the more delicate perfume of the pink-flowering thorn.
>
> From the corner of the divan of Persian saddlebags on which he was lying, smoking, as was his custom, innumerable cigarettes, Lord Henry Wotton could just catch the gleam of the honey-sweet and honey-colored blossoms of the laburnum, whose tremulous branches seemed hardly able to bear the burden of a beauty so flame-like as theirs; and now and then the fantastic shadows of birds in flight flitted across the long tussore-silk curtains that were stretched in front of the huge window, producing a kind of momentary Japanese effect, and making him think of those pallid jade-faced painters of Tokio who, through the medium of an art that is essentially immobile, seek to convey the sense of swiftness and motion. The sullen murmur of the bees shouldering their way through the long unmown grass, or circling with monotonous insistence round the dusty gilt horns of the straggling woodbine, seemed to make the stillness more oppressive. The dim roar of London was like the bourdon note of a distant organ.

Translated into contemporary English, this elaborate introduction might be condensed to read: "It was a summer afternoon, and the air smelled sweet. Lord Henry Wotton was chain smoking." Of course, this revision says very little. But when we look closely at Wilde's version, we must recognize that it does not say all that much more. And some of the things that it does say are questionable to say the least. Why would a painter have the curtains in his studio closed? And as cigarettes no longer seem as elegant as they did in 1891, one is left wondering how the laburnum could compete with all the tobacco.

Of the four sentences here, the average length is fifty-two words, with the second sentence weighing in at a whopping 119. Wilde would have defended himself by claiming that he was setting the scene, and the heaviness of the prose helps to suggest the rich and heavy atmosphere he is trying to evoke. But despite the wealth of detail we are given, we learn almost nothing which is relevant to the narrative. Does it matter, for example, that the woodbine in the garden was "straggling" or that the branches of the laburnum were "tremulous" or that the bees were "sullen"? Unfortunately not. The style of this passage has been arbitrarily applied, lacking any real connection with its subject. In pausing to describe the movement of a bee, another writer might manage to convey more than a decorative effect—to convey a parallel, somehow, between the observation of the natural world and the activities in which the story's characters are engaged. But Wilde seems unable to do this; his descriptions often seem as if they could be peeled off, leaving a stronger and more vigorous text behind.

The effect can be depressingly mechanical. One tremulous flamelike flower sounds very much like another—Wilde has an irritating tendency to re-use vocabulary. Within a relatively few pages, for example, we hear of "an exquisite violin," "exquisite knowledge," "exquisite disdain," "an exquisite day," "exquisite raiment," "exquisite taste," and "exquisite specimens." A similar predilection is shown for the words "graceful," "delicate," and "wonderful." Adjectives, in general, abound. Such prose as this is easily parodied.

In defending this style, Wilde argued that in prose "correctness should always be subordinated to

artistic effect and musical cadence; and any peculiarities of syntax that may occur in *Dorian Gray* are deliberately intended, and are introduced to show the
value of the artistic theory in question."[5] The artistic
theory to which he alludes rejected "modernity of
form" as "vulgarizing" and argued that beauty can be
found only in "the things that do not concern us."[6]
Certainly there is little in "the straggling woodbine"
that concerns us. And there is no question about
Wilde's belabored sentence structure having much in
common with modernity of form. Contrived though
this prose may now seem, it represents Wilde's attempt to emphasize the distinction between "art" and
"the prison house of realism."[7] He was determined to
keep reality at bay through, in his own words, "the
impenetrable barrier of beautiful style, of decorative
or ideal treatment."[8]

But there is more to conveying a sense of beauty
than simply listing the tremulous flowers in a garden.
As Lord Henry Wotton observes, "details are always
vulgar"—a dictum Wilde would have done well to
heed. As it is, he assaults his readers with great indi-
gestible chunks of detail, a process that culminates in
Chapter 11 in which Wilde lists, for the entire
chapter, every scent, every song, every jewel, and
every embroidery that Dorian Gray comes to admire.
Reading this chapter is like reading the catalogue for
an auction one will never attend.

Wilde is even unfaithful to his own aesthetic.
Although he dismissed those novelists who write of
"the sordid streets and hideous suburbs of our vile
cities,"[9] he himself takes us—for no apparent reason—
to the home of Sibyl Vane where we learn that "the
flies buzzed round the table, and crawled over the
stained cloth." Later we are brought into a waterfront
tavern complete with "fly-blown mirrors" and "greasy
reflectors of ribbed tin" illuminating a floor covered

with mud and spilled liquor. And what are we to make
of the description of Mr. Isaacs, the theater manager:

A hideous Jew, in the most amazing waistcoat I ever beheld
in my life, was standing at the entrance smoking a vile
cigar. He had greasy ringlets, and an enormous diamond
blazed in the center of a soiled shirt.

Aside from its obvious anti-Semitism, this passage is
coarse and melodramatic; it dates Wilde as surely as
the would-be lyricism of the more decorative lines.

Thus in addition to faulting Wilde for being, at
times, too precious, we must also charge him with occasionally slipping into the melodramatic. Could anyone have ever really spoken like Sibyl Vane:

He is called Prince Charming . . . Prince Charming, my
wonderful lover, my god of graces. But I am poor beside
him. Poor? What does that matter? When poverty creeps
in at the door, love flies in through the window.

Of course, there's more to Wilde than lines like these.
The conversation at Lady Agatha's luncheon, for
example—or later at the house party at Selby Royal—
is only a less-polished version of the brilliant dialogue
that Wilde perfected in *The Importance of Being
Earnest*. And, as we have seen, the novel is rich with
ideas.

Nonetheless, in our final verdict on *The Picture of
Dorian Gray*, we must conclude that interesting and
enjoyable though it may be, it is very much the work
of a writer who had yet to find himself. Both in its
theme and in its style the book is marked by that in-
consistency that springs from an inadequately defined
purpose. It has plot, and it has wit. But it is intellectually and stylistically immature.

3

Commercial Success:
Lady Windermere's Fan,
A Woman of No Importance,
and *An Ideal Husband*

As we turn to Oscar Wilde as a dramatist, we turn to that aspect of his career for which he is best remembered. For every reader who enjoys *The Picture of Dorian Gray*, there are a dozen who can recall one of the comedies that Wilde wrote in the early 1890s. His most famous play is, without question, *The Importance of Being Earnest*. His last and best play, this deserves separate consideration and will be discussed in the next chapter, after we have examined the three commercially successful plays that immediately preceded it: *Lady Windermere's Fan, A Woman of No Importance,* and *An Ideal Husband*.

Commonly grouped together as Wilde's "society comedies," these three plays reveal different degrees of success, and only one of them—*An Ideal Husband*—comes close to being great drama. But we can learn much from Wilde even when he is at his worst.

At the conclusion of the opening performance of *Lady Windermere's Fan*, the author was called for, and Wilde stepped forth upon the stage, announcing: "I am glad, ladies and gentlemen, that you like my play. I feel sure you estimate the merits of it almost as highly as I do myself." According to Frank Harris,

who was in the theater that night, the house rocked
with laughter. Whatever its flaws, there can be no
question that the play was a great success. At a time
when the purchasing power of the pound was much
higher than it is today, Wilde received £7,000 in royal-
ties from the first production alone.

The plot focuses around three principal characters
—Lord and Lady Windermere, a young couple who
have been married for only two years, and an older
woman of questionable reputation, Mrs. Erlynne.
Lady Windermere is famous for taking a high moral
tone, and her marriage is regarded as ideal. She learns
in the first act, however, that her husband has been
paying daily visits to Mrs. Erlynne—and also paying
her large sums of money. She draws the conclusion
that Mrs. Erlynne must be her husband's mistress.
Lord Windermere denies that this is so, but he ag-
gravates his wife's suspicions by insisting that she invite Mrs. Erlynne to her birthday ball, which is
planned for that very evening. When she refuses to do
so, Lord Windermere sends off an invitation in his
own hand. Lady Windermere threatens to strike Mrs.
Erlynne across the face with the fan she has just received from her husband as a birthday gift. As she
storms from the room, and the first act concludes,
Lord Windermere declares to the audience: "My God!
What shall I do! I dare not tell her who this woman
really is. The shame would kill her."

As we learn in Act II, Mrs. Erlynne is really Lady
Windermere's mother. Twenty years ago, she had
abandoned her husband and year-old child in order
to elope with her lover. Lady Windermere had grown
up believing that her mother was dead, when she was
actually living a life of pleasure on the Continent.
Threatening to reveal her true identity, Mrs. Erlynne
has been blackmailing Lord Windermere for the last
six months. She is determined to work her way back

into society and reasons that her path would be made clear if she were received in public by the fastidious Lady Windermere. Lady Windermere, of course, knows nothing of this, since her husband is determined to protect her from the truth. So far from having an affair with Mrs. Erlynne, Lord Windermere is merely trying to appease his mother-in-law in order to preserve his wife's self-esteem.

This rather unlikely plot is complicated by the unfolding of two separate courtships. Lord Darlington, a fashionable man–about–town, is determined to seduce the virtuous Lady Windermere, while Mrs. Erlynne, for her part, is determined to inveigle a proposal of marriage from the wealthy, but dissolute, Lord Augustus. Her presence at Lady Windermere's ball would establish her social acceptability—the one stumbling block to the marriage she desires.

When the curtain rises on the second act, we find ourselves at Lady Windermere's ball. Lady Windermere is still resolved to strike Mrs. Erlynne if she crosses her threshold, and considerable suspense is built up as the butler announces guest after guest and the confrontation is deferred. When Mrs. Erlynne arrives, Lady Windermere is paralyzed with indecision and drops her fan to the floor. For the remainder of the ball she seems reconciled to the presence of Mrs. Erlynne, and in any case, she is kept occupied by Lord Darlington, who pleads with her to elope with him. Lady Windermere turns him down, and Lord Darlington vows to leave England the following day. Shortly afterwards, however, Lady Windermere sees her husband leave the ballroom with Mrs. Erlynne. Convinced that the pair are continuing their affair under her own roof, she leaves a note for her husband explaining that she has decided to run away with Lord Darlington, who has by now left the party. Lady Windermere thereupon hurries off to Lord Darlington's home, and her note is discovered not by her husband but by Mrs. Erlynne.

Resolved to rescue her daughter from the scandal that seems about to break, Mrs. Erlynne rushes to Lord Darlington's flat, where she finds Lady Windermere waiting for him to return from his club. Pleading with her daughter to return to her husband, Mrs. Erlynne makes the most dramatic speech of the play, a speech that Wilde may well have made to his own critics:

You don't know what it is to fall into the pit, to be despised, mocked, abandoned, sneered at—to be an outcast! to find the door shut against one, to have to creep in the hideous byways, afraid every moment lest the mask should be stripped from one's face, and all the while to hear the laughter, the horrible laughter of the world, a thing more tragic than all the tears the world has ever shed. You don't know what it is. One pays for one's sin, and then one pays again, and all of one's life one pays. You must never know that.

And she concludes with admirable advice:

Go back Lady Windermere, to the husband who loves you, whom you love. You have a child Lady Windermere. Go back to that child who even now . . . may be calling to you . . . . Back to your house Lady Windermere—your husband loves you. But even if he had a thousand loves, you must stay with your child.

Lady Windermere bursts into tears and asks to be taken home.

Suddenly the women hear voices outside the door. Realizing that Lord Darlington is returning home with some friends, the two women hide behind a curtain in order to avoid discovery. Lady Windermere accidently leaves her fan in plain view, however, and her husband—who proves to be one of the Darlington party—immediately recognizes it. Believing that his wife

must be hiding somewhere upon the premises, Lord
Windermere demands an explanation and threatens a
search. At this moment Mrs. Erlynne steps forth from
behind the curtain and claims responsibility for the
fan, saying that she must have taken it by mistake.
Lord Augustus and Lord Windermere look upon her
with contempt, convinced that she must be having an
affair with Lord Darlington. As the third act draws to
a close, it seems that Mrs. Erlynne has destroyed her
own chance for advancement, but her self-sacrifice has
saved her daughter's reputation.

In the fourth and final act, we find Lady Windermere safely at home once again, her honor intact. Mrs.
Erlynne calls upon her in order to return her fan and
to announce that she has decided to leave London and
live abroad once again. Lady Windermere vows to tell
her husband the true story of the night before, but
Mrs. Erlynne makes her promise not to do so, arguing
that "love is easily killed." When Lady Windermere
agrees to remain silent, Mrs. Erylynne prepares to
leave. But she encounters Lord Augustus at the door.
Within minutes she succeeds in winning back his confidence, and the play concludes with the Windermeres
happily reunited and Mrs. Erlynne engaged to be
married.

If the comic potential of this plot is not readily
apparent, it is for good reason. It is not the sort of
story that can be taken lightly, treating as it does in-
fidelity, blackmail, and deceit. Both Mrs. Erlynne and
Lady Windermere speak with real passion, and the
exposure with which each is threatened would be ir-
retrievably ruinous. Wilde himself may have recognized that this "comedy" has a disturbingly serious
plot. The union of Mrs. Erlynne with Lord Augustus,
in the last fifty lines of the play, strikes one as a rather
desperate attempt to relieve the tension of the last
several acts in order to end on a light note. But it is an
arbitrary conclusion at best.

As a summary of the plot suggests, *Lady Windermer's Fan* is very much a play with a message. Its original title was *A Good Woman*, and the play explores what it means to be "good." Throughout the first act, it seems that Lady Windermere is a "good woman." We hear her described as such by other characters, an assessment with which she agrees:

You think I am a Puritan, I suppose? Well, I have something of the Puritan in me. . . . I lived with Lady Julia, my father's eldest sister, you know. She was stern to me, but she taught me, what the world is forgetting, the difference between what is right and what is wrong. *She* allowed no compromise. *I* allow of none.

It is impossible to overlook the air of complacency, however, which infects almost everything she has to say. Conventionally good women of this sort are not to be taken seriously. They are good only in the narrow sense that they are respectable, like the two young women we hear of early in the play—"such nice domestic creatures—plain, dreadfully plain, but so good —well, they're always at the window doing fancy work, and making ugly things for the poor." Women of this sort abound. "Why, I have met hundreds of good women. I never seem to meet any but good women. The world is perfectly packed with good women. To know them is a middle class education."

Lord Darlington urges Lady Windermere to be more tolerant. "I am afraid that good people do a great deal of harm in this world," he tells her. "It is absurd to divide people into good and bad." But she remains rigidly fixed to what she believes are her principles. We might sympathize with her refusal to invite Mrs. Erlynne to her ball. But when she vows to strike Mrs. Erlynne across the face and defends her intention on the grounds that "there is not a *good* woman in London who would not applaud me," she reveals herself to be both sanctimonious and vindictive.

Mrs. Erlynne, on the other hand, seems to be anything but "good." As the Duchess of Berwick tells it, "Many a woman has a past, but I am told that she has at least a dozen, and they all fit." Or as she is described by another guest at the birthday ball: "Looks like an edition de luxe of a wicked French novel, meant specially for the English market."[1] She is also described— by Lady Windermere—as "a woman who has neither mercy nor pity in her, a woman whom it is an infamy to meet, a degradation to know, a vile woman, a woman who comes between husband and wife."

But by the end of the second act, it becomes clear that whatever her indiscretions, Mrs. Erlynne is essentially "a good woman"—the good woman alluded to in the original title of the play. Protecting her daughter at the cost of her own reputation, Mrs. Erlynne reveals herself capable of generosity, love, and self-sacrifice.

When Lady Windermere learns the full extent of the service Mrs. Erlynne had done for her, she learns the basic message of the play. Although Lord Windermere is thoroughly disillusioned—"I thought she wanted to be good . . . I believed what she told me—I was mistaken in her. She is bad—as bad as a woman can be"—Lady Windermere knows better:

Arthur, Arthur, don't talk so bitterly about any woman. I don't think now that people can be divided into the good and the bad, as though they were two separate races or creations. What are called good women may have terrible things in them, mad moods of recklessness, assertion, jealousy, sin. Bad women, as they are termed, may have in them sorrow, repentance, pity, sacrifice. And I don't think Mrs. Erlynne a bad woman—I know she's not.

And in case the audience has missed the point, Wilde has Lady Windermere restate the theme a few moments later:

There is the same world for all of us, and good and evil, sin and innocence, go through it hand in hand. To shut one's eyes to half of life that one may live securely is as though one blinded oneself that one might walk with more safety in a land of pit and precipice.

The last line of the play is also hers. Speaking to Lord Augustus after he has announced his engagement to Mrs. Erlynne, Lady Windermere declares, "Ah! you're marrying a very good woman." And the audience is certain to agree. Although Mrs. Erlynne is adept at sounding glibly fashionable ("Repentance is quite out of date. And besides, if a woman really repents, she has to go to a bad dressmaker, otherwise no one believes in her. And nothing in the world would induce me to do that"), she is really the voice of reason throughout the play. She is far from perfect, but as she herself observes: "Ideals are dangerous things. Realities are better. They wound, but they are better."

Bearing this theme in mind, it comes as something of a surprise to find *Lady Windermere's Fan* dismissed, in some quarters, as no more than "fashionable trash."[2] Under its clever dialogue, the play reveals a strong strain of the melodramatic; its principal weakness is the way in which humor is expected to rise above a plot which is anything but funny. More often than not, the language of the play seems to be at odds with its subject. But *Lady Windermere's Fan* should not be seen as trivial. Whatever its flaws, the play reveals considerable talent, not only for dialogue and sound construction but also for reintroducing to the English stage at least a glimpse of the profound.

A Woman of No Importance is even more melodramatic than *Lady Windermere's Fan*. The title refers to a middle-aged woman, Mrs. Arbuthnot, who lives a secluded life in the country devoted to doing good works. Her son Gerald announces that he has been offered a post as private secretary to Lord Illingworth, a wealthy aristocrat who seems headed for an important diplomatic career. We learn in Act II, however, that twenty years earlier, Lord Illingworth had seduced and then abandoned a virtuous young woman. And—small world—it turns out to be the mother of the young man he has just hired as his secretary. He is, in short, Gerald's father, although he himself is unaware of their relationship.

Mrs. Arbuthnot tries hard to keep Gerald from accepting Lord Illingworth's offer. She is afraid that he will be corrupted, but she cannot adequately explain her fear, since she had raised Gerald to believe that his father was dead. The climax is reached at the end of the third act. The characters are all gathered at the home of Lady Hunstanton, who was originally responsible for introducing Gerald to Lord Illingworth. Lord Illingworth is intrigued by another guest, Hester Worsley, a self-consciously chaste American heiress. He tries to kiss her, and the horrified Miss Worsley runs to Gerald shrieking, "Oh! save me—save me from him." Gerald turns to Lord Illingworth and tells him, "You have insulted the purest thing on God's earth, a thing as pure as my own mother . . . . As there is a God in heaven, I will kill you!" At this point, Mrs. Arbuthnot is forced to intervene: "Stop, Gerald, stop! He is your own father."

In the fourth and final act, Gerald vows to make his mother marry Lord Illingworth. When Illingworth actually proposes to her, however, she refuses him with contempt. Gerald, in the meantime, is busy in the garden with Miss Worsley, who was so thrilled by the way he stood up for her that she has decided to marry him even though she is fabulously wealthy and he is virtually penniless. Thwarted in his evil plans, Lord Illingworth insults Mrs. Arbuthnot, and she is left sobbing on the sofa until Gerald and Hester return to announce their engagement.

The problem with this plot is that it depends upon a number of coincidences which are impossible to accept. It is hard to believe that a rich and arrogant nobleman would offer an important post to a provincial bank clerk. And then when it emerges that the clerk is really the illegitimate son of this very same noble lord—unbeknownst to either of them—the plot becomes even less credible. But perhaps the silliest aspect of the story is its conclusion. Crying "Child of my shame, be still the child of my shame!" Mrs. Arbuthnot explains that she refused Lord Illingworth's proposal because she likes things just the way they are. Poverty and disgrace agree with her, it would seem. She is proud that she has kept Gerald from inheriting his father's estates—presumably he is too good for that sort of thing. Unworldliness of this magnitude is very rare indeed, and one does not expect to find it in society as described by Oscar Wilde.

The characters we meet in this play are all vaguely familiar. Once again we have the woman with a past—although Mrs. Arbuthnot is far less sympathetic than Mrs. Erlynne—a woman given to black-and-white moral judgments, and, of course, a dandy. As in *Lady Windermere's Fan*, Wilde uses these diverse types to explore moral questions.

Lord Illingworth—a slightly more dapper, and sinister, version of Lord Darlington—claims that pleasure is the point of life: "One should sympathise with the joy, the beauty, the colour of life. The less said about life's sores the better." Above all else, it is important not to form moral judgments: "Taking sides is the beginning of sincerity, and earnestness follows shortly afterwards, and then the human being becomes a bore." He can be charmingly flip: "One can survive everything nowadays, except death, and live down anything except a good reputation," and he is likely to endear himself to his audience because of his wit. But as the outcome of the play reveals, he is at heart selfish, manipulative, and cruel.

Into the superficial society Lord Illingworth represents, Wilde plants an objective observer from abroad. Hester Worsley may be excessively serious, but she cannot be dismissed with a well-turned phrase. When she speaks at length, we see that she is no simple prig but a rebel with a cause. Her judgment of her fellow guests is a judgment on the fashionable audiences that flocked to be amused by Wilde:

You rich people in England, you don't know how you are living . . . . You shut out from your society the gentle and the good. You laugh at the simple and the pure. Living, as you all do, on others and by them, you sneer at self-sacrifice, and if you throw bread to the poor, it is merely to keep them quiet for a season. With all your pomp and wealth and art you don't know how to live—you don't know even that. You love the beauty that you can see and touch and handle, the beauty that you can destroy, and do destroy, but of the unseen beauty of a higher life, you know nothing. You have lost life's secret. Oh, your English society seems to me shallow, selfish, foolish. It has blinded its eyes, and stopped its ears. It lies like a leper in purple. It sits like a dead thing smeared with gold. It is wrong, all wrong.

This is a speech of real passion, and it reveals Wilde's characteristic ambivalence toward the glamor that another part of his nature could not help but crave. It is as if Wilde wants society to be both witty and good, glamorous and dependable, unaware that he cannot have it both ways.

A modern audience is also likely to be interested in the way in which Wilde makes Hester denounce society because of its hypocrisy towards women. In a relatively early denunciation of the much-discussed "double standard," Hester complains that men who have seduced women are welcomed by the same society that scorns the women who have been seduced: "Set a mark, if you wish, on each, but don't punish the one and let the other go free. Don't have one law for men and another for women."

Like Lady Windermere, however, Hester is inclined to be too severe. She is so busy condemning sinners that she fails to realize that sinners sometimes suffer and repent; she lacks a sense of compassion. It is Hester, after all, who announces "Let all women who have sinned be punished." And in conversation with Mrs. Arbuthnot, unaware that the woman with whom she is speaking had borne, in Gerald, an illegitimate child, Hester asserts that a woman who has sinned "shouldn't be allowed to come into the society of good men and women." What's more, "It is right that the sins of the parents should be visited on the children. It is a just law. It is God's law." To which speech Mrs. Arbuthnot responds with feeling, "It is one of God's terrible laws."

But like Lady Windermere, Hester Worsley learns to be more tolerant. Ultimately it is Hester who urges Mrs. Arbuthnot not to marry Lord Illingworth: "That would be a real dishonour, the first you have ever known. That would be a real disgrace: the first to touch you." When Hester thereupon reveals that she would like to marry Gerald, Mrs. Arbuthnot reminds her of her previous judgment: "But we are disgraced. We rank among the outcasts. Gerald is nameless. The sins of the parents should be visited on the children. It is God's law." But Hester has learned what Wilde would teach us all: "I was wrong. God's law is only Love."

The quality of the play cannot be a appreciated, however, if we focus only upon its plot and its theme. To this melodramatic story of abandonment and attempted rape, Wilde has fused—albeit not very successfully—some extraordinarily witty dialogue. The play is especially rich in epigrams, and we encounter many of its best lines with a sense of familiarity, so often have they been quoted: "Nothing succeeds like excess"; "The only difference between the saint and the sinner is that every saint has a past, and every

sinner has a future"; "Twenty years of romance make a
woman look like a ruin; but twenty years of marriage
make her something like a public building." His description of a fox hunt is especially memorable: "The
English country gentleman galloping after a fox—the
unspeakable in full pursuit of the uneatable." Lines
like these were meant to titillate, and titillate they did.
Their success depends as much upon their air of
mildly shocking irreverence as upon the clever manipulation of language.

But Wilde's humor does not rely exclusively upon
epigram. *A Woman of No Importance* is, on the
whole, less successful then *Lady Windermere's Fan*. In
at least one respect, however, it marks a real break-
through. We find in this play the first glimmer of the
sort of black humor Wilde would perfect in *The Importance of Being Earnest*. In the middle of the relatively predictable second and third acts, we find the
marvelously original Archdeacon and his offstage wife.
Consider the following dialogue:

LADY HUNSTANTON: I should so much like dear Mrs.
Daubeny to hear her on the violin. Ah, I forgot. Dear Mrs.
Daubeny's hearing is a little defective, is it not?

THE ARCHDEACON: Her deafness is a great privation
to her. She can't even hear my sermons now. She reads
them at home. But she has many resources in herself, many
resources.

LADY HUNSTANTON: She reads a good deal, I suppose?

THE ARCHDEACON: Just the very largest print. The
eyesight is rapidly going. But she's never morbid, never
morbid.

Lady Hunstanton is then drawn away by other guests,
but she and the Archdeacon come together again in
the next act:

LADY HUNSTANTON: My memory is getting so defective. Mrs. Daubeny has a wonderful memory, hasn't she?

THE ARCHDEACON: She used to be quite remarkable for her memory, but since her last attack she recalls chiefly the events of her early childhood. But she finds great pleasure in such retrospections, great pleasure . . . .

LADY HUNSTANTON: Well, I won't keep you from her. I have told Farquhar to put a brace of partridge into the carriage. Mrs. Daubeny may fancy them.

THE ARCHDEACON: It is very kind of you, but Mrs. Daubeny never touches solids now. Lives entirely on jellies. But she is wonderfully cheerful, wonderfully cheerful. She has nothing to complain of.

There is something wonderfully comic about this mindless good cheer in the face of decay. And the sensibility behind this humor is distinctly modern; as in the theater of the absurd, we laugh at death in the hope of keeping it from us.

Unfortunately, humor has entirely disappeared by the time we reach the last act. Like *Lady Windermere's Fan*, *A Woman of No Importance* is comedy in a formal sense; both explore the foibles of human nature and end with a happy resolution—marriage in each case. But the very element that adds substance to these plays—the moral undercurrent that makes them something more than clever entertainments—also tends to weaken their structure. Humor is ultimately at odds with plot, as if Wilde could not determine what he wanted to do—write comedy or melodrama. And this is especially evident in *A Woman of No Importance*. Each act becomes more didactic than the last, and by the end of the play, the comic is abandoned for the maudlin.

An Ideal Husband opened in London on January 3, 1895. Although considerably longer than either *Lady Windermere's Fan* or *A Woman of No Importance,* it proved to be an enormous success. When the Prince of Wales sent for Wilde on the opening night, the flat-

tered playwright remarked that he would have to cut
some of the scenes. "Pray do not take out a single
word," said the Prince, and Wilde was more than
happy to leave the play as it was. While a modern
audience is likely to be more critical, it cannot be denied that *An Ideal Husband* is much better crafted than
either of Wilde's earlier comedies. Indeed, no less a
judge than George Bernard Shaw was moved by this
work to pronounce Wilde "our only thorough playwright."[3]

The play centers around a group of characters
who have by now grown into easily recognizable
types. Once again we have a woman of high moral
principle—Lady Chiltern. We have a character with a
secret past (her husband, Sir Robert Chiltern), a
dandy (Lord Goring), and a fashionable woman of
questionable reputation, Mrs. Cheveley. But these
characters show a new degree of depth. If Lady Chiltern is a good woman, she is seldom so one dimen-
sional as Mrs. Arbuthnot. And if Lord Goring affects a
dandylike pose, he is much more complex than either
Lord Darlington or Lord Illingworth.

Sir Robert Chiltern is "the ideal husband" referred
to in the title of the play. Lady Chiltern can see in him
no wrong: "He is not like other men," she tells Lord
Goring. "Robert is as incapable of doing a foolish
thing as he is of doing a wrong thing." Lord Goring
knows better and argues,

I have sometimes thought that . . . perhaps you are a little
too hard in some of your views on life . . . . In every nature
there are elements of weakness, or worse than weakness
. . . . Nobody is incapable of doing a foolish thing. Nobody
is incapable of doing a wrong thing.

As the action of the play unfolds, this is precisely the
lesson that Lady Chiltern—like Lady Windermere before her—must learn.

Years earlier, when he was an ambitious young man serving as private secretary to a cabinet minister, Robert Chiltern had learned that the British government was about to purchase the Suez Canal. He sold this secret to a speculator three days before the news was made public, and was paid, for this tip, over one hundred thousand pounds—easily half a million dollars in today's currency. This sum formed the basis for his subsequent career. As the play begins, he is under secretary of state for foreign affairs, widely admired as a man of moral stature, and almost certainly destined to become prime minister one day.

Unfortunately, there exists against him one piece of evidence—the original letter advising purchase of Suez Canal stock. This letter has fallen into the hands of Mrs. Cheveley, an adventuress whom Wilde describes as "a work of art, on the whole, but showing the influence of too many schools." Mrs. Cheveley has invested heavily in a scheme to promote a canal in South America, a scheme Sir Robert is preparing to denounce, in the House of Commons, as a swindle. Mrs. Cheveley is determined to keep Sir Robert from making this speech; she demands that he suppress his report and say a few words to the effect that the canal, if completed, may be of great international value. Unless he agrees to do so, Mrs. Cheveley will make public the incriminating letter that she possesses, thus effectively ruining Sir Robert's career and his marriage to a woman who will allow no compromise with deceit.

Greatly troubled, Sir Robert agrees to do as he has been told, but then he is confronted by his wife, who tells him that she had known Mrs. Cheveley when they were girls at school together:

LADY CHILTERN: She was untruthful, dishonest, an evil influence on everyone whose trust or friendship she could win. I hated her, I despised her. She stole things, she was a thief. She was sent away for being a thief. Why do you let her influence you?

SIR ROBERT: Gertrude, what you tell me may be true, but it happened many years ago. It is best forgotten! Mrs. Cheveley may have changed since then. No one should be entirely judged by his past.

LADY CHILTERN: One's past is what one is. It's the only way by which people should be judged.

The irony of this exchange is that both characters are wrong. Mrs. Cheveley is no better than she was as a girl—if anything, she is much worse, and Lady Chiltern is right to judge her by her past. But in taking such an absolute position, in arguing that everyone should be judged by the past, she has condemned her own husband, unaware that he has a past that he has kept concealed from her.

Convinced that he will lose his wife's love if he tells her the truth, Sir Robert assures her that he has never done anything dishonorable and that he will make his original speech as planned. Unfortunately, the scandal cannot be contained. When Lady Chiltern tells Mrs. Cheveley, "Leave my house. You are unfit to enter it," Mrs. Cheveley strikes back:

Your house! A house bought with the price of dishonour. A house, everything in which has been paid for by fraud. Ask him what the origin of his fortune is! Get him to tell you how he sold to a stockbroker a Cabinet secret. Learn from him to what you owe your position.

Vowing once again to make her information public, Mrs. Cheveley leaves Sir Robert to the reproaches of his wife in a scene that reveals the essence of the play. Lady Chiltern takes refuge in theatrics:

Don't come near me. Don't touch me. I feel as if you had soiled me forever. Oh! what a mask you have been wearing all these years! A horrible, painted mask! You sold yourself for money . . . . And how I worshipped you! You were to me something apart from common life, a thing pure, noble, honest, without stain. The world seemed to me finer because you were in it, and goodness more real because you lived. And now—Oh, when I think that I made of a man like you my ideal, the ideal of my life!

Even a nineteenth-century audience would recognize that Lady Chiltern has gone too far. Because she demanded the impossible of her husband—perfection—she has catapulted from one extreme to another, from unreasoning adoration to unreasonable contempt. There is no question that Sir Robert has done a serious wrong. But our sympathies turn to him when he explains that he never wanted to be an ideal, that he would have preferred to be loved for what he is:

It is not the perfect, but the imperfect, who have need of love. It is when we are wounded by our own hands, or by the hands of others, that love should come to cure us—else what use is love at all? All sins, except a sin against itself, Love should forgive . . . . You made your false idol of me, and I had not the courage to come down, show you my wounds, tell you my weaknesses. I was afraid that I might lose your love, as I have lost it now . . . . And now what is there before me but public disgrace, ruin, terrible shame, the mockery of the world, a lonely, dishonoured death . . . . Let women make no more ideals of men! let them not put them on altars and bow before them, or they may ruin other lives as completely as you—you whom I have so wildly loved—have ruined mine!

There is, to be sure, an element of melodrama here. But the scene is nonetheless powerful and the lesson clear. Once again, we find Wilde condemning absolutes and pleading for tolerance in a world that is apt to be harsh.

At this point, the plot becomes increasingly complicated. Lord Goring had once urged Lady Chiltern to turn to him if she ever found herself in need of a friend. And now, at the beginning of Act III, he receives a note from her reading "I want you. I trust you. I am coming to you," from which he rightly deduces that Lady Chiltern has learned her husband's secret. As he prepares to receive her and urge her to stand by her husband, Lord Goring is interrupted by a visit from his father. Goring instructs his butler, "There is a lady coming to see me this evening on particular business. Show her into the drawing room when she arrives," and he retires offstage with his father. Mrs. Cheveley now appears, and believing that this must be the woman his employer is expecting, the butler ushers her into the drawing room. Once there, she discovers the letter Goring has just received from Lady Chiltern, which she takes as proof that they are having an affair. Sir Robert Chiltern now arrives upon the scene, anxious to have the advice of a man he respects. But when he discovers Mrs. Cheveley in Lord Goring's house, he is convinced that his best friend is in league with his worst enemy, and he leaves in disgust.

Mrs. Cheveley now makes an unexpected request. She tells Lord Goring that she will surrender Sir Robert's letter if Goring will agree to marry her. And here the already complex plot takes still another twist. We have known since Act I that Mrs. Cheveley has lost a diamond and ruby brooch. This brooch is now in Lord Goring's possession, and he shows it to her, asking if it is hers. She claims it with delight, and he fastens it to her arm, explaining that it was really designed as a bracelet with a secret spring. Once she has the bracelet on, Mrs. Cheveley cannot remove it because she does not understand how the spring works. Lord Goring knows how to work it because he had originally bought the bracelet as a gift for a cousin from whom it had been stolen ten years earlier. He threatens to expose Mrs. Cheveley as the thief unless she yields up Sir Robert's incriminating letter. She does so, but she holds fast to Lady Chiltern's letter, finding consolation in the thought that if she cannot ruin Sir Robert's career, she can at least ruin his marriage.

All of these complications are finally resolved in the fourth and last act. When Mrs. Cheveley sends Lady Chiltern's letter to Sir Robert, Sir Robert assumes that the letter has come to him direct from his wife. Believing that his wife is prepared to forgive him, he seeks her out and discovers that this is indeed the case. Determined to make the play end happily, Wilde omits any further mention of the wicked Mrs. Cheveley. Lord Goring proposes marriage to Sir Robert's younger sister and ward, and we are told that Sir Robert has been asked to join the Cabinet in recognition of his brilliant speech denouncing the South American canal scheme. Lady Chiltern kisses her husband and promises, "For both of us a new life is beginning." And on that happy note, the curtain falls.

If Lady Chiltern is able to forgive her husband, it is because she learns that she was wrong to expect him to be perfect. The notion of "an ideal husband" is introduced comically at first—a minor character complains: "My Reginald is hopelessly faultless. He is really unendurably so, at times! There is not the smallest excitement in knowing him." But we know that Wilde is serious in encouraging his audience to resist the temptation to romanticize. It is particularly dangerous to insist on ideals, if ideals mean an inability to compromise:

> SIR ROBERT: Arthur, I couldn't tell my wife . . . . She would have turned from me in horror . . .
> LORD GORING: Is Lady Chiltern as perfect as all that?
> SIR ROBERT: Yes; my wife is as perfect as all that.
> LORD GORING: What a pity!

To be perfect is to be rigid and incapable of human feeling. Life cannot be lived according to absolutes;

we must learn to be flexible and willing to change. Lady Chiltern boasts that she never changes, and even so unsympathetic a character as Mrs. Cheveley is moved to say, "Then life has taught you nothing . . . . I am sorry for you Gertrude, very sorry for you."

As late as Act IV, however, Lady Chiltern reveals an almost fatal rigidity. Although it is clear that her husband regrets his one and only sin, and although she recognizes that she loves him still, she urges him to retire from public life. Because his public life is based upon "a lie," it is his "duty" to give it up, regardless of his power for doing good so long as he is in office. But once again Lord Goring steps forward as the voice of tolerance:

You love Robert. Do you want to kill his love for you? What sort of existence will he have if you rob him of the fruits of his ambition . . . . Rather than lose your love, Robert would do anything, wreck his whole career, as he is on the brink of doing now. He is making for you a terrible sacrifice. Take my advice, Lady Chiltern, and do not accept a sacrifice so great. If you do, you will live to repent it bitterly. We men and women are not made to accept such sacrifices from each other.

Lady Chiltern is wise enough to accept this advice, thus ensuring a stronger and happier future for her marriage. She has learned not to demand an "ideal husband."

Returning to this theme on a lighter note in the final scene of the play, Wilde makes Lord Goring's father counsel the imminent bridegroom to become an "ideal husband." But Goring's young fiancée has the sense to declare:

An ideal husband! Oh, I don't think I should like that. It sounds like something in the next world. He can be what he chooses. All I want is to be . . . a real wife to him.

Feminists might well argue that women get the raw end of this deal, but it would be a mistake to see the play as urging women to forgive their husbands no matter what they do. If *An Ideal Husband* focuses upon the need to be tolerant of the shortcomings of men, it is only because Wilde had already made a similar plea for women in his two preceding plays. He urges men and women alike to accept one another as they are and not to place one another "on monstrous pedestals," because "we all have feet of clay, women as well as men."

The two men who figure the most prominently in this play deserve careful consideration. Sir Robert Chiltern is, as we have seen, a character with a past. But he is much more complex than either Mrs. Erlynne or Mrs. Arbuthnot. Mrs. Erlynne has more or less outlived her scandal; although she expresses remorse in the memorable confrontation with her daughter, she has put her past behind her in order to devote herself to gaining an untroubled future. Mrs. Arbuthnot, on the other hand, dwells almost exclusively in the past. Her sin was the single great event in her life, and she nurses its memory, determined to live a life of constant self-abnegation. If one woman is too little troubled by her past, the other is troubled too much, and compared to Sir Robert Chiltern, both are relatively one-dimensional.

Sir Robert is recognizably human. He is capable of wallowing in self-pity:

I sold, like a common huckster, the secret that had been intrusted to me by a man of honour. I thank heaven poor Lord Radley died without knowing that I betrayed him. I would to God I had died before I had been so terribly tempted, or fallen so low.

We know that this is insincere. Regardless of any remorse he may feel, he sees the past in proportion and is determined to fight to maintain his position in the world. When he is honest, he admits "I felt that I had fought the century with its own weapons, and won."

And when Lord Goring rebukes him for having been so weak, he refuses to respond with platitudes:

Weak? Oh, I am sick of hearing that phrase. Sick of using it about others. Weak? Do you really think, Arthur, that it is weakness that yields to temptation? I tell you that it requires strength and courage, to yield to. To stake all one's life on a single moment, to risk everything on one throw, whether the stake be power or pleasure, I care not—there is no weakness in that. There is horrible, terrible courage.

But then, reflecting upon the vulnerability of his success, he concludes, "I remember having read somewhere that when the gods wish to punish us they answer our prayers." This is no cardboard figure, but a real man feeling an intriguing mixture of grief and anger. He neither offends us with indifference nor bores us with hysterics, and it is satisfying to find him redeemed by the end of the play.

Because Sir Robert is basically good, there is no need for him to be publicly humiliated. But he has only narrowly escaped from a real danger, as Mrs. Cheveley reminds us. Speaking of the newspapers, she envisions what would eventually come to pass in Wilde's own life:

Think of their loathsome joy, of the delight they would have in dragging you down, of the mud and mire they would plunge you in. Think of the hypocrite with his greasy smile penning his leading article, and arranging the foulness of the public placard.[4]

The charge of public hypocrisy is repeated by Sir Robert, who reflects bitterly upon how he would be scorned by "men who, each one of them, have worse secrets in their own lives." And we should not be misled by the lightness of Lord Goring's response: "That is the reason they are so pleased to find out other people's secrets. It distracts public attention from their own."

Sir Robert Chiltern's fear of public ruin might

well be Wilde's own. The play was written only a year
before its author found himself in court, a time when
Wilde was afflicted with a strong sense of his own
impending doom. Describing *An Ideal Husband* in a
letter to a friend, Wilde observed: "It reads rather
well, and some of its passages seem prophetic of tragedy to come." But while Wilde clearly identified with
Sir Robert, it would be a mistake to see that character
as the sole voice of Wilde's point of view within the
play.

If as a popular public figure hovering on the brink
of disgrace Sir Robert finds himself in a position that
was analogous to Wilde's, Lord Goring represents the
way Wilde liked to see himself. Of all Wilde's dandies,
Goring is by far the most interesting. Although he
chooses to show himself as shallow to those who do
not interest him, he is, as we are allowed to see, both
wise and kind.

Wilde says that Goring is "clever, but would not
like to be thought so . . . . He is fond of being mis-
understood. It gives him a post of vantage." He likes
to stand apart from life in order to better understand
it, but he is also capable of action when those he loves
need help.

Throughout the play, we see two Lord Gorings:
one is the glib young man who likes to scandalize
dowagers at lengthy dinner parties; the other is the
loyal friend who never fails to offer wise counsel. He
can be irritatingly trivial—"To love oneself is the beginning of a life-long romance"—but this is, for the
most part, a manner that he assumes in order to avoid
sentimentality. He is easily embarrassed by the expression of feeling. When Sir Robert tries to thank him for
his help, he retreats, characteristically, into the facile:
"Ah! the truth is a thing I get rid of as soon as possible! Bad habit by the way. Makes one unpopular at
the club . . . ."

In Lord Goring, Wilde created a character very

much like himself. Like Wilde, Goring lies about his
age, claims to worship youth, is easily bored, and appears to be selfish. But as a recent critic has shown,
Goring

is also a kind of providence who settles all troubles by quick
brainwork and utter detachment. Outwardly a dandy and
an idler, he is inwardly a philosopher, even a man of action
and decision if need be. All Wilde's friends remarked that
in spite of his frivolous attitude towards life . . . . his advice
in mundane affairs was singularly shrewd, and each of these
characteristics is given to Goring.[5]

The philosopher would not be possible without the
dandy. It is the seemingly idle life that leaves the
dandy free to observe his fellow men, and observation
is the beginning of wisdom.

Thus both Lord Goring and Sir Robert Chiltern
should be seen as representing different aspects of
Wilde's own character. One represents the dandified
self, which sees itself as superior to social norms and
entitled to complete freedom; the other, the sinner
with a guilty conscience who admits that he has done
wrong but argues that he should not be punished.
Speaking in the person of Sir Robert, Wilde

admits that he has sinned in rejecting the mores of society.
He insists, however, that he has remained uncorrupted at
heart and begs society for pardon and acceptance. Speaking
as Lord Goring . . . . Wilde disdains that society and demands absolute freedom for the expression of the self. He
denies the existence of evil and good and maintains that
the only realities are ugliness and beauty.[6]

Like *The Picture of Dorian Gray, An Ideal Husband*
reveals the conflict of the divided self. Wilde wanted
to be loved and accepted by the very people he loved
to taunt. In simple terms, he did not know what he
wanted—the source, perhaps, of his personal misfor-

tune, but also the source of much that gives interest to his work.

Of the three plays discussed in this chapter, *An Ideal Husband* is unquestionably the most serious. Technically it is a comedy, because it ends happily. But there is very little humor in the play beyond an occasional epigram, and the business of the diamond bracelet is distinctly melodramatic. Nonetheless, *An Ideal Husband* shows considerable improvement over Wilde's earlier plays in both construction and characterization. If it lacks the brilliant dialogue one usually associates with Wilde, it clearly has the substance with which he is seldom credited. Wilde was to write only one more play, *The Importance of Being Earnest*. But within *An Ideal Husband*, there are moments of high drama that make one wonder what new directions Wilde might have pursued had his career not ended so precipitously. This is his best play but one.

It should now be possible to reexamine the standard critical evaluation of these three plays, which is that they have foolish and sentimental plots peopled with one-dimensional characters—a judgment that is softened only by the widespread recognition that the dialogue, at least, is often brilliant. There is an element of truth here, as there is in every commonplace. But Wilde is trickier than he looks at first glance.

Underlying much of the criticism of these plays is one simple complaint: Oscar Wilde is not realistic. It is true that many of Wilde's plots are highly contrived, and it is also true that many of his characterizations are stilted. The point we need to grasp, however, is that Wilde was not interested in being realistic. His world is deliberately artificial. Transparent plots and one-dimensional characters are not insurmountable obstacles to maintaining a sense of the artificial: indeed, one might argue that their very remoteness from the world as we know it helps to foster the atmosphere that Wilde sets out to create in reintroducing the comedy of manners to the English stage. In short, Wilde should be judged in terms of what he set out to do, not in terms of what held no interest for him. We should stop blaming him for not being Ibsen.

Moreover, because something is artificial, it does not necessarily follow that it is shallow. Unlikely though they may be, Wilde's plots nonetheless reveal values that deserve to be taken seriously. Each of these plays is designed to remind us that people are seldom what they appear to be. Each plot centers around a concealed sin that seems about to become exposed, and in each case we are asked to forgive the sinner. One might easily read these plays as a cry from Wilde's own heart—a plea to his audience to forgive his own sin when it is finally exposed.

Critics often fail to grasp that these plots helped make Wilde commercially viable. However stale they may seem to us, they nonetheless work as theater. Each play is built around a series of strong scenes, and each act ends with a strong curtain line. Wilde was working, after all, within the theater of the 1890s and had certain expectations to fulfill. His use of language was sufficiently original to startle the audience of the day; his use of relatively conventional plots provided that same audience with a reassuringly familiar framework for the paradoxical ideas it was being asked to digest. Wilde was as original as possible for his time—perhaps even too original, when one considers his personal fate. We should measure Wilde against the eminently forgettable melodramas of his period and not dismiss him because he was capable of exploiting elements of those melodramas for his own ends.

A careful examination of these plots reveals, however, that they are not as conventional as they may seem. Although Wilde used familiar situations, he con-

sistently managed to twist them about. One of the
situations in *Lady Windermere's Fan*, for example, is
the pattern of the long-lost child. But in this play, it is
the parent, not the child, who is lost. Then, although
the whole play seems to move towards a recognition
scene in which mother and daughter joyfully embrace
—in the tradition of countless melodramas—this never
comes to pass. And finally, the play includes a discovery scene that is actually a nondiscovery scene. We
expect Lady Windermere to be discovered in Lord
Darlington's rooms, but once again, our expectations
go unfulfilled. In short, the play "is built upon the
frustration or non-fulfillment of three of the most ancient and common theatrical devices imaginable.
Wilde has put it together by *not* completing traditional patterns."[7]

To a lesser extent, this pattern holds true for *A
Woman of No Importance*. Once again we find the
prominent use of a recognition scene, and in this case
the recognition is complete: Gerald learns that Lord
Illingworth is his father. But what follows thereafter
confounds our expectations. No joyful reunion results;
the penniless clerk does not become his father's heir as
we are clearly led to expect, especially after Lord
Illingworth calls upon Mrs. Arbruthnot to arrange
precisely that. Recognition leads not to a reunion
among the characters but to additional disarray. Here
is a family that cannot be drawn together. The other
standard plot that Wilde here incorporates revolves
around the courtship of two lovers of unequal rank.
The most traditional resolution of this situation in English literature is for the audience to discover that the
lovers really are of equal rank, as in *Tom Jones*. The
twist here is that Gerald wins Hester Worsley not because he has been recognized by his father but because he has the character to deny his father. Indeed,
our dissatisfaction at the end of this play is derived, at

least in part, by the way Wilde frustrates our expectations. We are prepared to see the principle characters resolve their conflict; we certainly expect Lord Illingworth at least to repent. But this is not the case—the characters refuse to do as we wish.

An Ideal Husband is the least conventional of these three plays. Despite some standard melodramatic devices, most noticeably the stolen diamond bracelet, Wilde's plot is original in at least two ways. Sir Robert and Lady Chiltern are reunited because the character who seems to be the most superficial proves to be the most substantial. Lord Goring is the voice of reason throughout the play, but whereas the standard choric voice would say "Tell the truth and accept the consequences," Lord Goring encourages his friends to put the truth behind them, and this prepares the way for a highly original ending. Sir Robert and Lady Chiltern do not retire to the country in order to live a life of quiet repentance. The scandal that has threatened Sir Robert's career never breaks; the villain is never punished. (Even Mrs. Cheveley gets to keep her diamond bracelet—she may never get it off her arm, but at least it's hers to keep.) So far from being humbled by the action of the play, the principals are prepared, as the final curtain falls, to move on to bigger and better things.

It thus becomes clear that Wilde has challenged one of the most basic conventions of nineteenth-century plotting: rewarding virtue and condemning vice. Each of these plays makes it apparent that the distinction between good and bad is almost impossible to draw. No one becomes "ideal," because, as Wilde reminds us, no one can be ideal. If Mrs. Erlynne is moved to rescue her daughter, she is still capable of lying to Lord Augustus. If Mrs. Arbuthnot feels repentance for her sin, she is nonetheless something of a hysteric and a nag who wants to keep her son all to herself. And when Lord Goring asks Sir Robert Chiltern if he has suffered much regret for what he has done, Sir Robert has the candor to say "No." Each of these characters is mixed. And in all cases, Wilde lets them have their own way. Mrs. Erlynne gets her man, Mrs. Arbuthnot frustrates Gerald's plea that she marry his father, and Sir Robert gets a seat in the Cabinet. Even Wilde's most disagreeable characters manage to get off scot-free. Lord Illingworth glides off to another party. And if Mrs. Cheveley's stock manipulation has been thwarted, she is nonetheless still at large, spared the exposure as a thief that a more conventional plot would surely have brought about.

If these plays are not completely successful, it is because of the very conflict which makes them so interesting. On the one hand we have the world of language—the world of intelligence and art; on the other hand, we have the world of orthodox moral opinion. Juxtaposed against the epigrams of a Lord Illingworth, we have the passionate propriety of a Hester Worsley. It is incredible that they can exist in the same play: It is as if one had crossed William Congreve with Jonathan Edwards—the combination does not work. Wilde is at his best when he can sustain the illusion of one world or another, be it the almost pure comedy of manners of the opening scenes of both *Lady Windermere's Fan* and *A Woman of Importance*, or the fine drama of *An Ideal Husband*. But in each play the illusion is allowed to break as Wilde shifts from one level to another. As a result, we tend to enjoy these plays in part but not in whole.

4

Exploring the Absurd:
The Importance of Being Earnest

Wilde claimed to have written *The Importance of Being Earnest* in less than three weeks during the summer of 1894. Consisting originally of four acts but cut to three during rehearsal, the play opened in London on February 14, 1895, only six weeks before Wilde found himself in court and his name removed from the placards that advertised his last great success. *The Importance of Being Earnest* is now widely recognized as one of the finest comedies in English. But like all true comedy, the play reveals a variety of disturbing undercurrents, as is suggested by its subtitle, "A Trivial Comedy for Serious People."

The play begins in the London apartment of Algernon Moncrieff, a young bachelor and something of a dandy. He is being visited by a friend whom he knows by the name of Ernest Worthing but whose real name is Jack Worthing. Jack lives in the country where he looks after his ward, Miss Cecily Cardew, a responsibility he is anxious to escape. As he himself explains:

When one is placed in the position of guardian, one has to adopt a very high tone on all subjects. It's one's duty to do so. And as a high moral tone can hardly be said to conduce very much to either one's health or one's happiness, in order to get up to town I have always pretended to have a younger brother by the name of Ernest, who lives . . . in London and gets into the most dreadful scrapes.

Using the pretext of helping this nonexistent brother, Jack makes frequent trips to London where—for no clear reason—he adopts the name of Ernest. And so he is known as Jack in the country and Ernest in town.

This confusion over names is important to the plot. Jack loves Gwendolen Fairfax, Algernon's cousin, and he proposes to her midway through the first act. She tells him that she is more than ready to marry him:

For me you have always had an irresistible fascination. Even before I met you I was far from indifferent to you . . . my ideal has always been to love some one of the name of Ernest. There is something in that name that inspires absolute confidence. The moment Algernon first mentioned to me that he had a friend called Ernest, I knew I was destined to love you.

In the absurd dialogue which follows, Gwendolen insists that she could only love a man named Ernest: "It is a divine name. It has music of its own. It produces vibrations." When Jack suggests that "Jack is also a nice name," Gwendolen will not hear of it: "I have known several Jacks, and they all, without exception, were more than usually plain." Jack decides, therefore, to be rechristened at once.

At this point, we are introduced to Gwendolen's mother, Lady Bracknell, who proceeds to interview Jack in order to see if he is a socially acceptable suitor. Jack explains that he does not know who his parents were. He had been adopted by the late Thomas Cardew, Cecily's grandfather, who gave him the name of Worthing "because he happened to have a first-class ticket for Worthing in his pocket at the time. Worthing is a place in Sussex. It is a seaside resort." Further inquiries lead Jack to admit that he was found in a

handbag in the cloakroom of Victoria Station. Lady
Bracknell cannot approve:

To be born, or at any rate bred, in a hand-bag, whether
it had handles or not, seems to me to display a contempt
for the ordinary decencies of family life that remind one
of the worst excesses of the French Revolution. And I
presume you know what that unfortunate movement led to?

Declaring that she cannot allow her only daughter "to
marry into a cloak-room, and form an alliance with a
parcel," Lady Bracknell forbids the match.

In the second act, the scene shifts to Jack's home
in the country. We meet his ward, Cecily, her governess, Miss Prism, and the local clergyman, Dr.
Chausuble. Into their world steps Algernon Moncrieff,
announcing himself as Jack's brother Ernest in order
to tease his friend. He immediately falls in love with
Cecily and prepares to make an extended visit. When
Jack returns from London, he is very much annoyed to
discover Algernon on the premises, and he tries hard
to get rid of him. But Algernon cannot be budged.
Instead of returning to London, he proposes to Cecily,
who gladly accepts him in terms almost identical to
what Gwendolen had already told Jack:

You must not laugh at me, darling, but it had always been
a girlish dream of mine to love someone whose name was
Ernest. There is something in that name that seems to
inspire absolute confidence. I pity any poor woman whose
husband is not called Ernest.

Thus we have two young women engaged to be married, each believing that she is engaged to Mr. Ernest
Worthing, who does not exist. Algernon decides that
he must get himself rechristened without delay, and he
leaves for the rectory, leaving Cecily alone in the
garden.

A guest is thereupon announced, and it proves to

be none other than Gwendolen Fairfax, who has decided to pay a surprise visit to the man she still hopes to marry. In conversation, Cecily confides that she is engaged to Ernest Worthing, and Gwendolen argues with her, believing that *she* is engaged to Ernest Worthing. This prompts a duel of wits between two well-armed opponents:

CECILY: Do you suggest, Miss Fairfax, that I entrapped Ernest into an engagement? How dare you? This is no time for wearing the shallow mask of manners. When I see a spade I call it a spade.

GWENDOLEN: I am glad to say that I have never seen a spade. It is obvious that our social spheres have been widely different.

Interrupted by the butler, they are forced to be polite and begin to discuss the country.

GWENDOLEN: Are there many interesting walks in the vicinity, Miss Cardew?

CECILY: Oh, yes, a great many. From the top of one of the hills quite close one can see five countries.

GWENDOLEN: Five counties! I don't think I should like that. I hate crowds.

CECILY: I suppose that is why you live in Town? . . .

GWENDOLEN: Personally I cannot understand how anybody manages to exist in the country, if anybody who is anybody does. The country always bores me to death.

CECILY: Ah! That is what the newspapers call agricultural depression, is it not?

This feud is ended when Algernon and Jack return upon the scene and admit to their real names. The two young women retreat into the house, declaring, "A gross deception has been practised on both of us." As Act II draws to a close, both couples are estranged.

When the curtain next rises, we are inside the house with Gwendolen and Cecily, who are rapidly growing bored. As soon as they are joined by the men,

Cecily unthaws long enough to ask Algernon, "Why did you pretend to be my guardian's brother?" Algernon replies, "In order that I might have the opportunity of meeting you." She decides that this explanation has to it "a wonderful beauty," and this prompts Gwendolen to put a similar question to Jack, and she is answered in similar terms. Both girls admit to being considerably mollified, but they tell their suitors: "Your Christian names are still an insuperable barrier."

At this point, Lady Bracknell reappears. She is displeased to discover that her nephew Algernon is engaged to marry someone she has never met. But she is won over when she learns that Cecily has a fortune of a hundred and thirty thousand pounds. Jack, however, forbids the match unless Lady Bracknell will allow Gwendolen to marry him. This Lady Bracknell refuses to do. But just as she is about to rush Gwendolen back to London—"Come dear, we have already missed five, if not six, trains. To miss any more might expose us to comment on the platform"—she is astonished to discover the existence of Miss Prism. It seems that twenty-eight years ago, Miss Prism was employed by Lady Bracknell's sister as a governess for her baby. The family had been amazed to discover, one day, nothing more in the baby's perambulator than "the manuscript of a three-volume novel of more than usually revolting sentimentality." The baby and Miss Prism had disappeared. "Prism," demands Lady Bracknell, "where is that baby?"

Miss Prism admits to having inadvertently left the baby in the cloakroom of Victoria Station, which makes Jack Lady Bracknell's nephew and Algernon's brothers. What's more, it emerges that his real name is Ernest. Jack and Gwendolen embrace, followed by Algernon and Cecily, and Miss Prism and Dr. Chasuble. Although Algernon's name remains Algernon—a slight wrinkle in the plot—Cecily conveniently overlooks this fact, and the play ends with the prospect of three marriages.

On the surface, at least, we are dealing with a cast of characters who are anything but attractive: they are mercenary, cynical, and unfeeling. Both male protagonists lie about their identity, and both of the leading women claim as their highest ideal the love of a proper name that gives off good vibrations. But strangely enough, there is nothing repulsive about these characters. They are redeemed by their wit and vitality. Thrust into a world in which innocent young girls contemplate the publication value of their diaries and worldly bachelors rush off to be baptized, we are led to suspend moral judgment and find humor in the unpredictable.

Our expectations are continually surprised. As Mary McCarthy has observed, "The London roué is artless simplicity beside the dreadnought society dowager, and she, in her turn, is out-brazened by her debutante daughter, and she by the country miss, and she by her spectacled governess."[1] Inversions of this sort are basic to the structure and purpose of the play. Of all Wilde's plays, *The Importance of Being Earnest* is the most wildly improbable. But the artificiality of the play serves an important purpose. By drawing us into a moral vacuum, Wilde is free to challenge almost everything we are likely to take seriously. Deliberately removed from the world as we know it, we are forced to reexamine the sort of values we normally take for granted.

To begin with, almost no one in this world is interested in telling the truth. Jack lies to Algernon; Algernon lies to Cecily; Cecily lies to Dr. Chasuble— and no one seems to mind. After all, illusion may be much more interesting than the truth.[2] As Gwendolen puts it, "In matters of grave importance, style, not sincerity, is the vital thing." And when Jack discovers that his real name is Ernest, he declares, "it is a terrible thing for a man to find out suddenly that all his life he has been speaking nothing but the truth." He asks Gwendolen if she can forgive him, and she responds, "I can. For I feel that you are sure to change."

Accordingly, conventional morality finds no advocate within the play. Everyone is much more concerned with being "interesting." When, for example, Cecily learns that she is to meet her wicked cousin Ernest, she observes: "I have never met any really wicked person before. I feel rather frightened. I am so afraid he will look just like everyone else." And when Algernon tries to assure her that he is not really wicked, she is clearly disappointed:

If you are not, then you have certainly been deceiving us all in a very inexcusable manner. I hope you have not been leading a double life, pretending to be wicked and really being good all the time. That would be hypocrisy.

Algernon is redeemed in her eyes not by virtue of his candor but by virtue of his style. "You've wonderfully good taste," Cecily finally concedes, "It's the excuse I've always given you for your leading such a bad life." Even Lady Bracknell, the most orthodox character in the play, agrees: "He has nothing, but he looks everything. What more can one desire?"

It therefore comes as no surprise to find religion taken very lightly. Its representative is the vaguely disreputable Dr. Chasuble, whose theology is strictly a matter of form:

My sermon on the meaning of the manna in the wilderness can be adapted to almost any occasion, joyful, or, as in the present case, distressing. I have preached it at harvest celebrations, christenings, confirmations, on days of humiliation and festal days.

(And what, we are left wondering at the conclusion of the play, has he been doing with Miss Prism during all those walks in the garden?) Or consider the way in which baptism is treated. Jack asks Chasuble, "I suppose you know how to christen all right?" Reassured on this score, he then proposes to drop by "to be christened myself, this afternoon, if you have nothing better to do." When Chasuble assures him that immersion will not be necessary—"Sprinkling is all that is necessary . . . . Our weather is so changeable"—Jack offers to "trot around about five." Algernon's attitude is equally flip. "I have not been christened in years," he observes, and when Jack tells him that once should be enough, he counters that "I know my constitution can stand it." Neither character gives to baptism the same passionate interest they lavish upon where to dine and what to eat.

In a similar vein, the idea of social reform—so beloved by the morally responsible—comes in for attack. Although Gwendolen declares that "we live . . . in an age of ideals," she undercuts this belief with irony: "The fact is constantly mentioned in the more expensive monthly magazines." Miss Prism is more straight forward: "I am not in favour of this modern mania for turning bad people into good at a moment's notice." And Cecily is just as skeptical. "I don't quite like women who are interested in philanthropic work. I think it is so forward of them." The following exchange with Algernon can be seen as a parody of the worn-out convention in which the virtuous young heroine reforms the dissipated rake:

ALGERNON: This world is good enough for me, cousin Cecily.
CECILY: Yes, but are you good enough for it?
ALGERNON: I'm afraid I'm not that. That is why I want you to reform me. You might make that your mission, if you don't mind, cousin Cecily.

CECILY: I'm afraid I've not the time, this afternoon.

ALGERNON: Well, would you mind my reforming myself this afternoon?

CECILY: That is rather Quixotic of you. But I think you should try.

ALGERNON: I will. I feel better already.

CECILY: You are looking a little worse.

The humor in this scene has many layers. We laugh, in the first place, because of the way in which the characters have reversed roles: the innocent country maiden sounds more cosmopolitan than the jaded man-about-town. We also laugh at the idea of reform as something that can be undertaken in an afternoon. But ultimately we laugh at the value of reform in itself: to reform is to conform, which is precisely what we do not want these characters to do. If Algernon is said to be "looking a little worse" because of his good intentions, it is because he is being untrue to himself. His strength of character lies in his lack of character; he is interesting because he is unconventional. As such, he provides a welcome relief from a society that is becoming depressingly mechanical, a society in which engagements should be determined by "the proper average that statistics have laid down for our guidance" and marriage made impossible without certificates of "birth, baptism, whooping cough, registration, vaccination, confirmation, and the measles; both the German and the English variety."

In order to remain uncontaminated by modern social values, one should reject education that is designed as "improving." Lady Bracknell observes that she does "not approve of anything that tampers with natural ignorance." She would certainly disapprove of the education that has been inflicted upon Cecily, whose studies have been grimly serious. Her assignments are hopelessly dull:

Cecily, you will read your Political Economy in my absence. The chapter on the Fall of the Rupee you may omit. It is somewhat too sensational. Even these metallic problems have their melodramatic side.

Fortunately, "in England . . . education produces no effect whatsoever," and Cecily remains a model of common sense. "I know perfectly well, she tells us, "that I look quite plain after my German lesson." And so she goes triumphantly her own way, discarding her textbook for her diary and having a thoroughly good time.

Like Cecily, Gwendolen regularly protests against abstract ideas. When Jack asks her if she could love him if his name were not Ernest, she replies: "Ah! that is clearly a metaphysical speculation, and like most metaphysical speculations has very little reference to all the actual facts of real life, as we know them." And in a later exchange, she speaks even more forcefully. When Jack asks if she can doubt his love, she responds:

I have the gravest doubts upon the subject. But I intend to crush them. This is not the moment for German scepticism.

Underlying these lines is the quiet recognition that intellectual speculation presents a real threat to a good complexion (a metaphor, more or less, for a comfortable life). It is not that thought is worthless, but that it is disturbing and unsettling. Because we live "in an age of surfaces," as Lady Bracknell puts it, anything that disturbs the tranquility of the surface must be banished. If one has doubts, one must be like Gwendolen and "put them down."

Ultimately, Wilde turns the critique of cleverness even against himself. The following exchange mocks the manner that Wilde so carefully cultivated:

ALGERNON: All women become like their mothers. That is their tragedy. No man does. That is his.
JACK: Is that clever?
ALGERNON: It is perfectly phrased! and quite as true as any observation in civilized life should be.
JACK: I am sick to death of cleverness. Everybody is

clever now-a-days. You can't go anywhere without meeting
clever people. The thing has become an absolute public
nuisance. I wish to goodness we had a few fools left.

ALGERNON: We have.

JACK: I should extremely like to meet them. What do
they talk about?

ALGERNON: The fools? Oh! about the clever people,
of course.

JACK: What fools![3]

The irony here is twofold. In the first place, Jack recognizes that cleverness can be tiring, and this is, to an
extent, a clever observation. People who are obsessed
with cleverness are indeed fools. But the humor of the
scene is finally at Jack's expense: Fools discuss clever
people, Jack discusses clever people, therefore Jack is
a fool.

Running throughout scenes of this sort is a consistent theme: one can be too clever for one's own good.
Knowledge can be corrupting, intelligence can lead to
despair. If Algernon prefers the "perfectly phrased" to
the profound, it is because he realizes that it is dangerous to probe deeply into the meaning of things. He
defends what he says on the grounds that it is "as true
as any observation in civilized life should be." Civilized life, as we know it, cannot take the truth. In
order to keep anarchy at bay, we must learn to take
things lightly.

George Bernard Shaw complained that *The Importance of Being Earnest* was Wilde's "first really heartless play."[4] If this seems to be so, it is because the
characters all believe that feelings must be taken as
lightly as ideas. With the world crumbling around our
feet, there is a tremendous temptation to elevate the
importance of love and marriage into a sort of cosmic
last resort. Wilde refuses to allow this. He blocks any
retreat into the sentimental by ridiculing the institu-

tions to which we are apt to cling the most desperately.

In the first scene of the play, we are told that marriage "is not a very interesting subject." Shortly afterwards, Jack announces that he intends to propose to Gwendolen. Algernon is disappointed by the news: "I thought you had come up for pleasure? . . . I call that business." And he goes on to explain:

I really don't see anything romantic in proposing . . . . Why, one may be accepted. One usually is, I believe. Then the excitement is over. The very essence of romance is un-certainty. If I ever get married, I'll certainly try to forget the fact.

We soon discover, however, that modern women are shrewder than Algernon realizes. Although Gwendolen claims to have fallen in love with Jack even before she met him—a situation that ridicules the idea of love at first sight by carrying it one step further back—she is all business when it comes to marriage. When Jack tries to propose to her, she treats him like a backward child.

JACK: We must get married at once. There is no time to be lost.

GWENDOLEN: Married, Mr. Worthing?

JACK: Well . . . surely. You know that I love you, and you led me to believe, Miss Fairfax, that you were not absolutely indifferent to me.

GWENDOLEN: I adore you. But you haven't proposed to me yet. Nothing has been said at all about marriage. The subject has not even been touched on.

JACK: Well . . . may I propose to you now?

GWENDOLEN: I think it would be an admirable op-portunity. And to spare you any possible disappointment, Mr. Worthing, I think it only fair to tell you quite frankly beforehand that I am fully determined to accept you.

JACK: Gwendolen!

GWENDOLEN: Yes, Mr. Worthing, what have you got to say to me?

JACK: You know what I have got to say to you.

GWENDOLEN: Yes, but you don't say it.

JACK: Gwendolen, will you marry me. (*Goes on his knees.*)

GWENDOLEN: Of course I will darling. How long you have been about it! I am afraid you have had very little experience in how to propose.

JACK: My own one, I have never loved anyone in the world but you.

GWENDOLEN: Yes, but men often propose for practice. I know my brother Gerald does. All my girlfriends tell me so.

There are several things to be realized about this exchange. In the first place, it is evident that whatever their shortcomings, men are innocents compared to women. For all this experience in the world, Jack is helpless before Gwendolen, who has no question in her mind about what is owed to her. Her feelings are not engaged by the prospect of marriage; she is exclusively concerned with making sure that the proposal be made according to proper form—it is a ritual that she must pass through, and as long as it must be done, it must be done correctly. Her insistence on form, her determination to see Jack go down on his knees and make a model proposal, is at once amusing and disheartening. We enjoy the scene as a parody of romantic ritual, but in the process, we find ourselves laughing at romance itself. Gwendolen seems so clever, and Jack so foolish, that we are almost convinced that form matters more than feeling.

It is impossible to imagine either Gwendolen or Cecily dying for love. When her mother forbids her to marry Jack, Gwendolen is perfectly philosophical. "I may marry someone else, and marry often," she tells the befuddled Jack, but nothing "can alter my eternal devotion to you." And in a similar scene, Cecily rejects the idea of waiting for one's true love:

I hate waiting even five minutes for anybody. It always
makes me rather cross. I am not punctual myself, I know,
but I do like punctuality in others, and waiting, even to be
married, is quite out of the question.

Witty and engaging though they may be, Wilde's her-
oines are nonetheless out for themselves.

Free as they are of feeling, Wilde's characters
take family life no more seriously than romance. Jack
can pretend to his ward that he has a brother living in
London, and Algernon feels no hesitation in pretending to be that brother. Miss Prism believes that the loss
of a manuscript is as important as the loss of a child.
And Lady Bracknell, that hardheaded paragon of
common sense, sees family life as little more than a
matter of convenience. After grilling Jack about his income, she observes: "Now to minor matters. Are your
parents living?" When Jack tells her that he has lost
both of his parents, Lady Bracknell retorts: "Both? . . .
That seems like carelessness." Unfazed by Jack's admission that he was found in a cloakroom in Victoria
Station, Lady Bracknell urges Jack "to try and acquire
some relations as soon as possible, and to make a definite effort to produce one parent, of either sex, before
the season is quite over." Family is important, but no
more so than the clothes that one wears—one might
acquire a family just as one shops for a wardrobe.

And because they are free of feeling, these characters are also free to laugh at death. The scene in
which Jack appears to announce the death of his nonexistent brother is marked by Miss Prism's unsympathetic response: "What a lesson for him! I trust he will
profit by it." Similarly, when Algernon announces the
death of his mythical friend Bunbury, Lady Bracknell
tells him that she is glad "that he made up his mind at
the last to some definite course of action." Mourning
would be absurdly out of place in this world. When
Lady Bracknell visits a newly widowed friend, she is

delighted to report, "I never saw a woman so altered; she looks quite twenty years younger." In a society that has insulated itself from all normal emotion, death is the ultimate joke.

In short, Wilde has taken us into a world in which nothing matters. Almost everything that traditionally is taken seriously—ranging from love to death—has been dismissed as inconsequential, the subject of humor but not of reverence. We can agree with Shaw that there is much that is heartless in the play, but it would be a mistake to go so far as to see it as "essentially hateful . . . a real degeneracy produced by his debaucheries."[5] Wilde's apparent heartlessness is really the cold objectivity of a surgeon. If Wilde cuts away conventional values, he does so for a purpose.

A growing number of critics have come to see *The Importance of Being Earnest* as an early example of existential drama. Morris Freedman, for example, describes the play as:

an account of the search of several young persons for meaning in a society extraordinarily reluctant, even impotent, to assign importance to anything except the superficial. The dominant atmosphere, as in Sartre's *No Exit*, as in the settings of Beckett, is boredom, emptiness, a despair of experiencing genuine feeling.[6]

And David Parker argues that "lurking always in the depths of the play is a steady contemplation of Nothingness."[7]

Many scenes support this interpretation. Consider the following dialogue:

ALGERNON: Do you know it is nearly seven?
JACK: Oh! it always is nearly seven.
ALGERNON: Well, I'm hungry.
JACK: I never knew you when you weren't . . . .
ALGERNON: What shall we do after dinner? Go to a theatre?

> JACK: Oh no! I loathe listening.
> ALGERNON: Well, let us go to the Club?
> JACK: Oh, no! I hate talking.
> ALGERNON: Well, we might trot round to the Empire at ten?
> JACK: Oh, no! I can't bear looking at things. It is so silly.
> ALGERNON: Well, what shall we do?
> JACK: Nothing!
> ALGERNON: It is awfully hard work doing nothing.

On one level this scene works as a simple satire of two overly indulged young men who are easily bored. We see them as children who do not know what to do, and Wilde is clearly making a comment on the habits of the leisure class they represent. But there is also an awareness here of what might be called the bankruptcy of experience—the way in which nearly everything eventually loses its appeal to those who live long enough. Nothing lasts but nothingness, and Algernon is absolutely right when he observes, "It is awfully hard work doing nothing."[8] When we no longer have diversions to fill our empty lives, we are forced to confront an infinite void, and this is, indeed, hard work.

Occasionally, the dialogue comes precariously close to the desperate. Although the tone may be light and frivolous, we catch glimpses of a world that is anything but funny:

> ALGERNON: I love hearing my relations abused. It is the only thing that makes me put up with them at all. Relations are simply a tedious pack of people, who haven't got the remotest knowledge of how to live, nor the smallest instinct about when to die.
> JACK: Oh, that is nonsense!
> ALGERNON: It isn't!
> JACK: Well, I won't argue the matter. You always want to argue about things.

ALGERNON: That is exactly what things were originally made for.

JACK: Upon my word, if I thought that, I'd shoot myself.

Denying the existence of absolutes, Algernon advances a point of view that is recognizably modern, a point of view before which Jack is helpless. He can defend himself only by dismissing as "nonsense" and "absurd" anything that threatens the stability of the world as he knows it. He can offer no counter-arguments of his own, and the vehemence of his denial—"if I thought that, I'd shoot myself"—makes us take Algernon all the more seriously. In all his encounters with Jack, Algernon remains coolly reasonable, and he regularly gets the last word.

ALGERNON: I love scrapes. They are the only things that are never serious.

JACK: Oh, that's nonsense, Algy. You never talk anything but nonsense.

ALGERNON: Nobody ever does.

Nobody speaks "sense" because nothing makes "sense" —the carefully ordered world it was once possible to believe in no longer exists. We have moved into the world of the absurd, a world in which everything can be argued but nothing can be resolved.

Because nothing retains fixed value, that which is traditionally considered trivial is no less important than that which is customarily considered serious. Consider the speech in which Jack sums up his complaint against Algernon:

This afternoon, during my temporary absence in London . . . he obtained admission to my house by means of the false pretense of being my brother [S]. Under an assumed name he drank, I've just been informed by my butler, an entire pint bottle of Perrier-Jouet, '89; a wine I was especially reserving for myself [T]. Continuing his disgraceful deception, he succeeded in the course of the afternoon in alienating the affections of my only ward [S]. He subsequently stayed to tea, and devoured every single muffin [T].

"Alienating affection" is no more important than eating all the muffins, for the simple reason that nothing ultimately has any meaning at all. The reversals between S—the serious—and T—the trivial—almost always produce a laugh. But there is more than humor here; there is the modern idea that what is called meaning is only a matter of perception, since everything is part of a continuum which lacks any purpose.

If the somber implications of the play are not immediately clear, it is because *The Importance of Being Earnest* is, on an immediate level, a very funny play. Despite all its serious undercurrents, it is ultimately good humored. Wilde does not rage against the absurd, like many a more fashionable existentialist— he finds too much pleasure in simply poking fun at it. If there are no absolutes and no moral certainties, there is at least wit—and pleasure for those who know how to find it.

5

Mannered Morality:
The Happy Prince **and** *A House of Pomegranates*

Despite a growing consensus that Wilde deserves to be taken seriously, critics have tended to dwell on those aspects of his work that reflect the wit and decadence with which one usually associates his name. No area of Wilde's work has been more consistently slighted than his fairy tales, in part, I suspect, because they offer inconvenient evidence that Wilde is more complex than he looks at first glance.

Originally published in two volumes—*The Happy Prince* in 1888, and *A House of Pomegranates* in 1891 —these stories reveal an uneasy blend of the moral and the fantastic. There are nine stories altogether— five in the first volume and four in the second. They have a number of features which make them characteristically Wilde's. But taking them in the order in which they first appeared, let us begin our analysis with a summary of each.

"THE HAPPY PRINCE"

Set upon a column overlooking the city he once ruled stands a beautiful statue of the Happy Prince, covered with gold leaf and fitted with precious stones. One night, shortly before winter, a swallow lands at his feet, seeking shelter before continuing on its flight south. It is startled to discover that the Happy Prince is crying. The statue explains that he is called the Happy Prince because he had done nothing but dance and play when he was alive. Now that he is dead, however, and set high above the city, he sees all the misery he had done nothing to relieve when it was in his power to do so.

Over the next three days, the statue asks the swallow to help him help his people. He orders it to remove the precious stones with which he is set, including his two sapphire eyes, and distribute them to the poor. When the swallow has done so, the Prince urges it to leave for Egypt before winter sets in. But the swallow refuses to abandon the Prince: "You are blind now," it tells him, "so I will stay with you always."

Even after the snow begins to fall, the swallow remains faithful to the Prince, singing to him during the day and at night removing pieces of gold leaf to give to the poor. Eventually the swallow realizes that it is going to die from the cold; it kisses the Prince goodbye and falls dead at his feet, prompting the statue's heart to break in two.

The townspeople are dismayed to find the statue looking so shabby. The Mayor complains: "The ruby has fallen out of his sword, his eyes are gone, and he is golden no longer . . . in fact, he is little better than a beggar." The statue of the Happy Prince is pulled down and melted in a furnace, all but its heart, which will not melt and is thus thrown into a heap of garbage with the dead swallow.

But virtue does not go unrewarded. When God asks one of His Angels to bring Him the two most precious things in the city, the Angel returns with the dead bird and the statue's heart. "You have rightly chosen," said God, "for in my garden of Paradise this little bird shall sing for evermore, and in my city of gold the Happy Prince shall praise me."

"The Nightingale and the Rose"

A student is passionately in love with a young woman who has promised to dance with him only if he presents her with a red rose. There are no red roses in his garden, however, and he loudly bemoans his fate. A nightingale hears his lament, and she decides, "Here indeed is the true lover . . . . What I sing of, he suffers; what is joy to me, to him is pain." She decides to help the student and flies around the garden in order to find at least one red rose. She finds white roses and yellow roses, but the red rose bush is barren; the frost has nipped it buds. The bush explains that there is only one way it can be brought to yield a rose:

If you want a red rose . . . you must build it out of music by moonlight, and stain it with your heart's-blood. You must sing to me with your breast against a thorn. All night long you must sing to me, and the thorn must pierce your heart, and your life-blood must flow into my veins, and become mine.

The nightingale does so that very night, pressing its breast against the thorn and singing more beautifully, and more frantically, as she grows weaker. At dawn, she lies dead in the grass, but the bush has produced a lovely red rose.

When he wakes at noon, the student discovers the rose and brings it to the girl he loves. She responds by telling him, "I am afraid it will not go with my dress . . . and besides, the Chamberlain's nephew has sent me some real jewels, and everybody knows that jewels cost far more than flowers." The student is very much annoyed, and he throws the rose into the gutter. He decides that love is "a silly thing" and "not half as useful as Logic." He thereupon returns to his room and devotes himself to a great dusty book.

"The Selfish Giant"

For seven years, the Giant has been away visiting his friend the Cornish ogre. "After the seven years were over he had said all that he had to say, for his conversation was limited." He returns to his own castle and is upset to discover that, in his absence, local children had formed the habit of playing in his garden. He chases the children away and builds a high wall around his property. "My garden is my own garden," he declares, "anyone can understand that, and I will allow nobody to play in it but myself." He posts a sign that reads "Trespassers will be Prosecuted," and the children are forced to play in the road.

Because the Giant has been selfish, the spring refuses to visit his garden, and winter reigns there for over a year. But then the Giant wakes one morning to the sound of birds singing outside his window. When he looks outside, he discovers that the children had crept back into his garden through a hole in the wall; they are sitting in all the trees, and every tree in which a child sits is full of beautiful blossoms. Only in one corner of the garden is it still winter. There is a little boy standing there, but he is too small to climb into a tree.

The Giant immediately realizes that he had been wrong to force the children from his garden:

How selfish I have been . . . now I know why the Spring would not come here. I will put that poor little boy on the top of the tree, and then I will knock down the wall, and my garden shall be the children's playground for ever and ever.

When he steps outside, however, the children are frightened and all run away—all but the little boy who had been unable to climb the tree: "His eyes were so full of tears that he did not see the Giant coming." The Giant picks him up and puts him in a tree, which immediately breaks out into blossom. The other children see that the Giant is no longer wicked, and they return to the garden, which is now more beautiful than ever.

There is, however, no sign of the small boy whom the Giant had put in the tree. Years pass, and the Giant continues to hope that he will once again see the child who had led him away from selfishness. One winter morning, when he is quite old, the Giant looks out his window and sees:

a tree quite covered with lovely white blossoms. Its branches were all golden, and silver fruit hung from them, and underneath it stood the little boy he had loved.

The Giant rushes to the child and finds nail prints upon his hands and feet. He asks who has harmed the child and is told that "these are the wounds of Love." The Giant kneels down before the child—who is, we may infer, the Christ child—and is told that he is about to enter Paradise. That afternoon, when the children arrive to play in the garden, they find the Giant lying dead beneath a tree.

"The Devoted Friend"

A number of animals are discussing the nature of friendship. A linnet asks a water rat what it means to be "a devoted friend." The water rat replies, "What a silly question! I should expect my devoted friend to be devoted to me, of course." This prompts the linnet to tell the story of an honest little fellow named Hans.

Hans works hard for a living, raising wonderful flowers that he takes to market to sell. He earns enough money to support himself through most of the year, but in the winter when there are no flowers, he is often cold and hungry.

Hans has a friend, a very large friend named Hugh the Miller, who is quite rich. So devoted to Hans is the Miller "that he would never go by his garden without leaning over the wall and plucking a large nosegay, or a handful of sweet herbs, or filling his pockets with plums and cherries if it was the fruit season." He justifies this behavior on the grounds that "real friends should have everything in common," but he never gives Hans anything in return. Even in the winter, when he knows that Hans is suffering, the Miller never moves to help the friend to whom he is supposedly so devoted. Sitting comfortably before his fire, he tells his wife, "When people are in trouble they should be left alone, and not bothered by visitors."

Come spring, the Miller goes to visit Hans. He learns that Hans has been forced to sell his wheelbarrow in order to buy food, and he offers to give Hans a wheelbarrow of his own:

It is not in very good repair; indeed, one side is gone, and there is something wrong with the wheel-spokes; but in spite of that I will give it to you. I know it is very generous of me, and a great many people would think me extremely foolish for parting with it, but I am not like the rest of the world. I think that generosity is the essence of friendship, and besides, I have got a new wheelbarrow for myself.

The Miller expects a great deal in return for this offer. He begins by helping himself to all of Hans's best flowers and a plank of wood that Hans had hoped to use himself. The next day, the Miller appears with a large sack of flour which he wants Hans to carry for him to market. Hans tries to tell him that he is busy, but the Miller retorts: "Well, really, I think that, considering that I am going to give you my wheelbarrow, it is rather unfriendly of you to refuse." Hans is mortified and quickly agrees to carry the flour to market. It is a long trip, and Hans is lying in bed exhausted when, early the next morning, the Miller arrives to

demand that Hans come and repair the roof of his
barn. Once again, Hans neglects his own responsibili-
ties in order to help his friend.

Finally, the Miller appears one stormy night and
asks Hans to fetch the doctor for his young son who
has fallen off a ladder. Because the doctor "lives so far
away, and it is such a bad night . . . it would be much
better if you went instead of me." He reminds Hans of
the promised but still undelivered wheelbarrow, and
Hans sets out to find the doctor in the midst of a
terrible storm. Although he manages to fetch the doctor, Hans loses his way home. He drowns in a pool of
water into which he accidentally stumbles, and his
body is discovered the next day. There are many
mourners at his funeral, the chief among them being
the Miller, who explains that he has experienced a
great loss—he no longer has a way to dispose of his
broken-down wheelbarrow.

"THE REMARKABLE ROCKET"

A variety of fireworks have been assembled for the
celebration of a royal marriage. Principal among them
is a very conceited rocket that speaks "with a very
slow, distinct voice, as if he was dictating his mem-
oirs." He explains that he is "a very remarkable Rocket,
and come of remarkable parents." He observes that
the king's son is lucky to be married on the same day
he will be let off and boasts that he knows no equal:
"The only thing that sustains one through life is the
consciousness of the immense inferiority of everybody
else, and this is a feeling I have always cultivated."
Moreover, he expects to be the center of everyone's
attention:

I am always thinking about myself, and I expect everybody else to do the same. That is what is called sympathy.
It is a beautiful virtue, and I possess it in a high degree.

The Rocket is so moved by his own magnificence that he bursts into tears and becomes so wet that he cannot be used when it is his turn to be let off. All the other fireworks are a great success, but the Rocket is discarded as refuse. His vanity is so great, however, that he cannot recognize what has happened to him. When workmen come to throw him away, he pretends that they are an official deputation which he must receive with "becoming dignity," and he looks more supercilious than ever. And when he is thrown into a mud puddle, he decides that it must be "some fashionable watering-place, and they have sent me to recruit my health. My nerves are certainly very much shattered, and I require rest."

Eventually he is seized upon by a couple of boys who are looking for kindling. They lay him on their fire, but he is so wet that he does not go off until after they have fallen asleep. As he finally shoots into the sky, he succeeds in frightening a goose. Vain and silly to the end, he observes, as he goes out, "I knew I should create a great sensation."

"The Young King"

A young princess secretly marries a "young man of marvelous and foreign beauty" and has a child by him. She dies shortly thereafter, and the child is raised in the forest by a peasant and his wife. Sixteen years later, the king sends for the child, his grandson, so that he can acknowledge him as his heir.

The story begins on the eve of the young king's coronation. We are told that he has "a strange passion for beauty"; when he sees beautiful jewels and fine fabrics, he reveals a "fierce joy." "Like one who was seeking to find in beauty an anodyne from pain, a sort of restoration from sickness," the young king seems to

have abandoned himself to the worship of physical
splendor:

It was said that a stout Burgomaster . . . had caught sight
of him kneeling in real adoration before a great picture
that had just been brought from Venice, and that seemed
to herald the worship of some new gods. On another
occasion he had been missed for several hours, and after a
lengthened search had been discovered in a little chamber
in one of the northern turrets of the palace gazing, as one
in a trance, at a Greek gem carved with the figure of
Adonis.

At midnight, he goes to sleep, and he dreams three
dreams. In his first dream, he sees gaunt and haggard
weavers working at their looms. He is told:

In war . . . the strong make slaves of the weak, and in
peace the rich make slaves of the poor. We must work to
live, and they give us such mean wages that we die. We
toil for them all day long, and they heap up gold in their
coffers, and our children fade away before their time, and
the faces of those we love become hard and evil. We tred
out the grapes, and another drinks the wine. We sow the
corn, and our own board is empty. We have chains though
no eye beholds them; and are slaves, though men call us
free.

To his horror, the young king then discovers that these
workers are intent upon weaving the robe that he is
supposed to wear at his coronation. He wakes, but
soon dreams again.

    In his second dream, the young king finds himself
upon a galley pulled by slaves. They reach a small
bay, and the youngest of the slaves is seized upon by
the overseers. His ears and his nose are filled with wax,
a large stone is tied around his waist, and he is sent
into the sea in order to search for pearls. He dives
many times, and each time he comes to the surface, he
brings with him a beautiful pearl:

Then the diver came up for the last time, and the pearl that he brought with him was fairer than all the pearls of Ormuz, for it was shaped like the full moon, and whiter than the morning star. But his face was strangely pale, and as he fell upon the deck the blood gushed from his ears and nostrils. He quivered for a little, and then he was still.

The slave's body is thrown overboard, and the master of the galley laughs. Examining the pearl, he announces that it shall be set into the scepter of the young king. The young king cries out in his sleep; he wakes, but soon begins to dream again.

In his third and final dream, the young king finds himself in a dim wood "hung with strange fruits and beautiful poisonous flowers." He comes upon a great crowd of men toiling in a dried-up river bed. He watches as they all die. "And out of the bottom of the valley crept dragons and horrible things with scales, and the jackals came trotting along the sand, sniffing up the air with their nostrils." The young king weeps and asks what the men had been searching for. He is told by a pilgrim that the men had been digging for rubies for the crown of a king. "For what king?" he asks. And he is handed a mirror in which he sees his own face.

When he wakes from this dream it is morning. His robe, scepter, and crown are brought in to him so that he may ready himself for his coronation. But remembering his dreams, he tells the assembled lords, "Take these things away, for I will not wear them." He bathes himself in clear water and dons the simple clothes he had worn in the forest. For his scepter he takes out a rude shepherd's staff, and for his crown he wears a spray of wild briar.

He leaves the palace and makes his way toward the cathedral. Along the way he is jeered by the crowd, and when he arrives at the cathedral, the bishop urges him to return to the palace and "put on raiment that beseemeth a king." The young king responds by kneeling before an image of Christ and bowing his head in prayer.

At this moment, a group of nobles breaks into the cathedral with drawn swords. "Where is this dreamer of dreams," they cry, determined to slay the young king for bringing shame upon the state. The young king rises up at the foot of the altar in order to meet them.

And lo! through the painted windows came the sunlight streaming upon him, and the sunbeams wove around him a tissue that was fairer than the robe that had been fashioned for his pleasure. The dead staff blossomed, and bare lilies that were whiter than pearls. The dry thorn blossomed, and bare roses that were redder than rubies. . . . He stood there in the raiment of a king, and the gates of the jeweled shrine flew open, and from the crystal of the many-rayed monstrance shone a marvelous and mystical light. He stood there in the king's raiment, and the glory of God filled the place, and the saints in their cavern niches seemed to move.

The people fall down upon their knees in awe, and the bishop declares, "A greater than I hath crowned thee."

"The Birthday of the Infanta"

A great celebration has been organized in honor of the twelfth birthday of the Infanta, the daughter of the King of Spain. Sitting on a "gilt and ivory chair" in a "long pavilion of purple silk," she is entertained by a tight-rope walker, a magician, and a puppet show. The climax of the festivities, however, is a dance performed by a horribly grotesque dwarf who is unconscious of his own deformities:

When the children laughed, he laughed as freely and as joyously as any of them, and at the close of each dance he made them each the funniest of bows, smiling and nodding at them just as if he were really one of themselves, and not a little misshapen thing that Nature, in some humorous mood, had fashioned for others to mock at.

The Infanta is fascinated by him, and at the conclusion of his performance she throws to him a beautiful white rose that had adorned her hair. She commands that the dwarf dance for her again after she takes her siesta.

The dwarf believes that the Infanta must love him, and he runs around the palace garden filled with the hope that she will come and live with him in the forest. Impatient to see her again, the dwarf decides to look for her in the palace. He wanders through a series of rooms, each more beautiful than the last, until he enters a room with a large mirror—something that he had never previously seen. He does not realize, at first, that he is gazing at his own reflection, but thinks that the creature he sees staring at him is "the most grotesque monster he had ever seen." When he finally understands that he is looking at his own self, he falls sobbing to the floor. Self-discovery has led to despair. He now knows that "it as at him that all the children had been laughing, and the little Princess who he had thought loved him—she too had been merely mocking at his ugliness, and making merry over his twisted limbs."

The Infanta enters the room and sees the dwarf "lying on the ground and beating the floor with his clenched hands, in the most fantastic and exaggerated manner." She laughs and applauds, pronouncing his acting to be even funnier than his dancing.

Suddenly the dwarf gives a curious gasp and becomes perfectly still. The Infanta is very much annoyed that the show has stopped. The dwarf, we learn, has died of a broken heart. The Infanta frowns and commands: "For the future let those who come to play with me have no hearts."

"THE FISHERMAN AND HIS SOUL"

A young fisherman catches a mermaid in his net one day. She is so beautiful that he falls in love with her. He agrees to set her free on condition that she come and sing to him whenever he calls.

Every evening after that, the mermaid rises out of the water and sings to the fisherman so beautifully that his nets are always full, for the fish are enchanted by her song. As the days go by, however, the fisherman neglects his nets, for he comes to care for nothing but the mermaid. He begs her to marry him, but she replies: "Thou hast a human soul . . . . If only thou wouldst send away thy soul, then could I love thee."

The fisherman decides to do just that. "Of what use is my soul to me?" he asks himself. "I cannot see it. I may not touch it. I do not know it." He consults the local priest as to how he may lose his soul, and the priest sends him away, telling him that there is "no thing more precious than a human soul" and that he is mad to want to part from his. The fisherman then tries to sell his soul to the merchants gathered in the marketplace, but they show no interest. "Of what use is a man's soul to us?" they ask. "It is not worth a clipped piece of silver."

But the fisherman then remembers that there is a witch who lives in a cave near the shore. He forces her to help him lose his soul. She pleads "Ask me anything but that!" but ultimately gives him a special knife, and tells him that if he stands with his back to the moon and tells his soul to leave him as he cuts his shadow from around his feet, he will have his wish.

The fisherman's soul begs to be allowed to dwell within him. When the fisherman refuses, his soul says to him:

If indeed thou must drive me from thee, send me not forth
without a heart. The world is cruel, give me thy heart to
take with me.

But the fisherman responds that his heart belongs to
the mermaid. He cuts his shadow from around his feet,
and his soul rises up before him, telling him, "Once
every year I will come to this place, and call to thee."
The fisherman responds by plunging into the sea,
where he is embraced by the mermaid.

After a year has gone by, the soul comes down to
the shore and calls to the fisherman. It tells him of its
adventures during the past year—how it had traveled
to the East and found there the Mirror of Wisdom,
stolen it from the temple in which it had rested, and
preserved it in a secret place. "Suffer me to enter into
thee, and none will be as wise as thou." But the fisherman replies, "Love is better than Wisdom," and returns to the mermaid.

After the second year is over, the soul returns to
the fisherman and tells him how it has traveled to the
south, where it has discovered the Ring of Riches. If
the fisherman will come out of the sea and rejoin his
soul, then he will be richer than all the kings of the
world. But the fisherman responds, "Love is better
than Riches." And once again the soul goes off alone.

After the third year, however, the soul tempts the
fisherman with beauty. It tells him of a marvelous
dancing girl, and remembering that the mermaid cannot dance, the fisherman leaves the sea. He says to
himself: "It is but a day's journey, and I can return to
my love."

The soul then leads the fisherman on a long journey. On the first day it commands him to steal a silver
cup from a booth in a bazaar; on the second day it
demands that he strike a young child, and on the third
day it tempts him to slay a merchant who has given
him hospitality. The fisherman does what he is told to

do, but he does not like it. He asks his soul why it
has made him do these things. And the soul tells him:
"When thou didst send me forth into the world thou
gavest me no heart, so I learned to do all these things
and love them."

The fisherman realizes that his soul has become
evil, and he vows to bind his hands and seal his lips, if
necessary, to keep from doing the soul's bidding. He
returns to the seashore and calls to the mermaid, but
she does not answer. Although his soul continues to
tempt him, first with the pleasure of evil and then with
the power of good, the fisherman stays by the water's
edge, where he calls to the mermaid every day. Eventually, the mermaid's body is washed up on the shore,
causing the fisherman's heart to break. Through this
break, the soul is able to enter once again into him.
And in the morning, the fisherman is found dead on
the beach with the body of the mermaid in his arms.

The priest declares that the fisherman has been
slain by God's judgment, and he orders that his body
and the body of the mermaid be buried in a desolate
field. From the ground in which they are buried, there
spring strangely beautiful flowers that, when they are
used to decorate the altar, inspire the priest to speak
"not of the wrath of God, but of the God whose name
is Love." Although the flowers never bloom again, the
priest has learned to be more forgiving. He goes to the
sea "and blessed the sea and all the wild things that
are in it." As the story ends, we are told, "All the things
in God's world he blessed, and the people were filled
with joy and wonder."

"THE STAR CHILD"

Two woodcutters are making their way home through
the forest on a bitterly cold night. They see a star fall
nearby and rush to it in the hope of discovering a pot

of gold. But when they arrive on the spot, they find not gold but a small child wrapped in gold cloth. One woodcutter argues that the child should be left to die, as they are both too poor to raise it. But his companion argues that this would be evil, and he brings the child to his home and gives it food that might otherwise have fed his own children.

The Star Child, as he comes to be called, grows into a thoroughly mean and selfish but incredibly beautiful boy who sticks reeds into the eyes of animals and throws stones at beggars. One day, when he is ten years old, there comes to the village a beggar woman who recognizes him as her own child. Although she is able to prove that she is indeed his mother, she is scorned by the Star Child, who tells her: "I am no son of thine, for thou art a beggar, and ugly, and in rags." He insists that she leave him alone and refuses to kiss her when she agrees to leave, saying that he would sooner kiss a toad or an adder.

The woman leaves the village, and the Star Child rejoins his companions. The other boys in the village now refuse to play with him, however, because he has suddenly become "as foul as the toad, and as loathsome as the adder." When he sees his reflection in a well, the Star Child realizes that he has been physically transformed as a punishment for his sin. He vows to wander the world over in order to search for his mother and to beg for her forgiveness.

For three years he wanders without finding "love nor loving-kindness nor charity . . . but it was even such a world as he had made for himself in the days of his great pride." One evening, he comes to the gates of a city, and the soldiers who are standing guard there sell him as a slave to an old man who proves to be an evil magician.

The magician brings the Star Child to his home and locks him in the dungeon. In the morning, he tells the child to go to the forest; hidden there are three pieces of gold, one red, one yellow, and one white. The magician orders the boy to bring him the piece of white gold, telling him that he will be whipped if he fails to do as he has been told.

The Star Child searches all over the forest, but he cannot find the piece of gold. At sunset, however, he discovers a hare caught in a hunter's trap. He takes pity on it and sets it free. "Surely thou hast given me freedom," says the hare, "and what shall I give thee in return?" The Star Child tells the hare of his quest for the white gold, and the hare is able to lead the boy directly to it.

The Star Child makes his way back to the city, delighted that he will be able to please his master. But at the city gates he meets a leper who says, "Give me a piece of money, or I must die of hunger." The boy takes pity on the leper and gives him the piece of gold. When he returns to his master emptyhanded, he is beaten and thrust unfed back into the dungeon.

In the morning, the magician comes to him and tells him to go back to the forest for the piece of yellow gold. Once again the Star Child searches in vain all day, and once again he is led to the gold by the hare at sunset. Upon his return to the city, he once again takes pity on the leper, who waits at the city gates, and the boy gives him his piece of gold. When he returns to the magician, he is beaten and loaded with heavy chains.

The next day, the magician commands the boy to return to the forest and bring to him the piece of red gold hidden there, vowing to set him free if he does so but to slay him if he fails. The hare once again leads the child to the piece of gold, and once again the boy gives it to the leper.

But now that he has shown charity for the third time, a great change takes place. The Star Child recovers his physical beauty, and the people of the city bow down before him. He is led to the palace of a king, and the priests and high officers of the city proclaim: "Thou art our lord for whom we have been waiting, and the son of our King."

The Star Child denies that he is the son of a king, and he argues that he is unworthy to rule the city because he had denied his own mother. At this moment he sees his mother standing in the crowd beside the leper he had helped. He kneels down at his mother's feet, and washes them with his tears, as he prays:

Mother, I denied thee in the hour of my pride. Accept me in the hour of my humility. Mother, I gave thee hatred. Do thou give me love. Mother, I rejected thee. Receive thy child now.

His mother and the leper both bid him to rise. And when he does so, he sees that they are truly a king and queen. They lead him into the palace, where he is crowned, and until his death, he rules over the city with wisdom and justice.

It is readily apparent that these stories advocate a consistently moral point of view. Each is designed to reveal the ugliness of a particular vice or the beauty of a particular virtue. Selfishness ("The Nightingale and the Rose," "The Selfish Giant," "The Devoted Friend"), vanity ("The Remarkable Rocket," "The Star Child"), heartlessness ("The Birthday of the Infanta," "The Fisherman and His Soul"), and self-indulgence ("The Young King") are all shown to be wrong. It we wish to find redemption from these sins, we must learn to be more open and generous. Like the Selfish Giant, we must break down the walls with which we surround ourselves; like the Happy Prince and the Star Child, we should give of ourselves even if it hurts.

The Happy Prince is called "happy" only because

he lived his life in isolation from his fellow man and thus knows nothing of suffering. Like the Spanish Infanta (or the young king before his redemption), he has lived entirely within his palace and its grounds. It is only after he is dead that he realizes an important truth: "more marvelous than anything is the suffering of men and women. There is no Mystery so great as suffering." Story after story emphasizes that it is wrong to close one's eyes to this suffering, and we find within them a growing concern for the poor. In the early stories, the poor tend to be vaguely picturesque—in "The Happy Prince," for example, the first two beneficiaries of the statue's generosity are both artists of a sort: a seamstress "embroidering passion-flowers on a satin gown" and a playwright living in a garret. But by the second volume of stories, Wilde has extended his sympathy to workers, slaves, lepers, and dwarfs.

Wilde argues that our values are misplaced. One of his most prevalent themes is that beauty, art, and wealth have little importance. Throughout "The Happy Prince," our sympathies are entirely with the statue and the swallow; Wilde shows that the precious stones and gold leaf that make the statue aesthetically pleasing are valuable only insofar as they may help to relieve the misery of men. Beauty that serves no higher purpose is apt to be corrupting, as we see in three other stories: "The Young King," "The Star Child" and "The Birthday of the Infanta."

When we first meet the young king, with his "strange passion for beauty," he seems given over to a life of sensual gratification. He is sprawled out "on the soft cushions of his embroidered couch, lying there, wild-eyed and open mouthed." As we watch him worship "a Greek gem carved with the figure of Adonis," escorted by a bevy of "slim, fair-haired Court pages," it seems likely that he will become as corrupt as Dorian Gray. But he learns, through his dreams, that the luxuries that adorn his palace could not exist were it not for human suffering. Although his robe, crown, and scepter are "more beautiful . . . than aught he had ever seen," he finds his redemption in their denial.

The Star Child is also saved from a vain obsession with beauty, in this case his own. We are told early in the story that "every year he became more beautiful to look at . . . . Yet his beauty did him evil. For he grew proud, and cruel, and selfish." It is only after he loses his beauty that he is capable of repenting for what he has done. Self-denial leads, once again, to the emergence of a better self.

In "The Birthday of the Infanta," however, the principle character remains unredeemed. Although of all the "slim Spanish children . . . the Infanta was the most graceful of all," she is, at the end of her story, more heartless than ever, curling her lips with "pretty disdain" as she watches the death of one who had loved her. Our sympathy is with the ugly dwarf, and we come to see that there is something corrupt in the heavy beauty of the Spanish court, where even nature seems artificial and overwrought:

The purple butterflies fluttered about with gold dust on their wings . . . the pomegranates split and cracked with the heat, and showed their bleeding red hearts. Even the pale yellow lemons, that hung in such profusion from the mouldering trellis and along the dim arcades, seemed to have caught a richer colour . . . and the magnolia trees opened their great globe-like blossoms of folded ivory, and filled the air with a sweet heavy perfume.

There is something almost sinful about this garden; the key words in its description—"split," "cracked," "heat," "bleeding," "pale," "mouldering," "dim," "sweet," and "heavy"—all suggest a world that is over-ripe or over-tired.

The dwarf stands in sharp contrast to the artificiality of the court. His element is nature:

For though he had never been in a palace before, he knew a great many wonderful things. He could make little cages out of rushes for the grasshoppers to sing in, and fashion the long-jointed bamboo into the pipe that Pan loves to hear. He knew the cry of every bird . . . . He knew the trail of every animal.

There can be no question but that we are meant to prefer the dwarf and his world, to the Infanta and her court. And we find here another of the themes that link Wilde's stories together: the superiority of the natural over the artificial.

Of course, it must be admitted that Wilde's conception of nature is highly fanciful, populated as it is with mermaids, fauns, anthropomorphic animals, and sentimentally inclined birds. Nonetheless, a surprising number of the fairy tales reveal sympathy for what Wilde calls "the wild things." In "The Fisherman and His Soul," for example, the priest is redeemed when he comes to accept all "the pagan things God suffers to wander through His world." Early in the story, he condemns the wild because it threatens him:

Accursed be the Fauns of the woodland, and accursed be the singers of the sea! I have heard them at night-time, and they have sought to lure me from my beads. They tap at the window, and laugh. They whisper into my ears the tale of their perilous joys. They tempt me with temptations, and when I would pray they make mouths at me. They are lost . . . . For them there is no heaven nor hell, and in neither shall they praise God's name.

But at the end of the story, he is inspired by flowers he has never seen before and "spake not of the wrath of God, but of the God whose name is Love." He blesses the fauns "and the little things that dance in the woodland, and the bright-eyed things that peer through the leaves" filling the people with "joy and wonder." He has learned, in short, that God can be found in all His creations.

We find a comparable association between God and nature in "The Young King." Redemption is signaled when the young king dons the simple clothes he had worn in the forest. After his transfiguration in the cathedral, "no man dared look upon his face, for it was like the face of an angel." And when the wild briar with which he has been crowned bursts into bloom, the roses are redder than rubies, and "whiter than fine pearls were the lilies."

Wilde's reference to "the God whose name is Love" is characteristic. During the years in which he wrote these stories, Wilde was becoming increasingly interested—as one of his best biographers has observed—"in the personality of Jesus Christ, an interest which increased every year until at length he almost identified himself with Christ and often spoke in parables."[1] Christ appears only once in the stories—in "The Selfish Giant." But the themes we have detected in the stories as a whole—the importance of charity, tolerance, and love—may be seen as a reflection of Wilde's growing interest in Christianity.

But Wilde's attitude towards love is complex. It figures prominently in many of the stories, and it is recognized as an important virtue. On the other hand, it is frequently associated with pain. When the Selfish Giant meets the Christ child, he is told that His wounds are "the wounds of Love." The nightingale suffers a prolonged and painful death for the sake of love, but this proves that her sacrifice is in vain. The swallow's love for the Happy Prince leads it to die at his feet, prompting the statue's heart to break in two. After he falls in love with the Infanta, the dwarf dies of a broken heart. And in "The Fisherman and His Soul," the mermaid dies after she is abandoned by the fisherman, and the fisherman dies of grief after he discovers her body.

Wilde's ambivalence toward love may be related to his ambivalence toward women. Many of the women in these stories are portrayed as incapable of love. In "The Happy Prince," a young man tries to speak to his love of the stars; she responds by saying, "I hope my dress will be ready in time for the Stateball." The girl who demands a red rose in "The Nightingale and the Rose" cannot recognize its value when it is presented to her. The Spanish Infanta demands, "Let those who come to play with me have no hearts." And the mermaid makes her love conditional upon the fisherman giving up his soul. It may be no accident that Wilde's most attractive characters—the Happy Prince, the Selfish Giant, little Hans, the young king, and the Star Child—are all bachelors.

It must be acknowledged that, despite their strong moral content, many of Wilde's fairy tales have an underside that is distinctly unnerving. This is most clearly evident in their conclusions: Wilde often goes out of his way to warn us that, even in fairy tales, it is hard to live happily ever after. Consider, for example, the conclusion of "The Star Child." The story seems headed for a happy ending; the Star Child has been rewarded for his self-denial. The second to last paragraph sees him become a prince. Moreover:

Much justice and mercy did he show to all, and the evil Magician he banished, and to the Woodcutter and his wife he sent many rich gifts, and to their children he gave high honour. Nor would he suffer any to be cruel to bird or beast, but taught love and loving-kindness and charity, and to the poor he gave bread, and to the naked he gave raiment, and there was peace and plenty in the land.

A more conventional tale would conclude at this point. But Wilde adds one more paragraph:

Yet ruled he not long, so great had been his suffering, and so bitter the fire of his testing, for after the space of three years he died. And he who came after him ruled evilly.

"The Fisherman and His Soul" ends with a similar retreat. After the priest has blessed the sea and filled the people with "joy and wonder," we expect the story to conclude on an affirmative note. But the last two lines emphasize defeat:

Yet never again in the corner of the Fuller's Field grew flowers of any kind, but the field remained barren even as before. Nor came the Sea-folk into the bay as they had been wont to do, for they went to another part of the sea.

It is impossible to overlook the sense of failure that permeates these stories. In "The Remarkable Rocket," failure is treated comically—we feel that the rocket deserves to fail because it had been so vain and silly. But this is an exception; for the most part, we regret the way in which essentially sympathetic characters are defeated before the story is over.

Almost invariably, the character with whom we have been encouraged to sympathize is eventually dispatched by the author's pen. The swallow in "The Happy Prince," the nightingale in "The Nightingale and the Rose," little Hans in "The Devoted Friend," the dwarf in "The Birthday of the Infanta," and the Star Child in the story that bears his name are all allowed to die. Occasionally, the virtuous are rewarded in a life after death, as in "The Happy Prince" and "The Selfish Giant." But in other stories, death seems to be triumphant, and the virtuous disappear, leaving only cruelty in their stead, as in "The Nightingale and the Rose," "The Devoted Friend," "The Birthday of the Infanta," and "The Star Child."

Resolutions of this sort make it clear that Wilde was not writing for the entertainment of children. Although they are filled with types of characters that would be familiar to children from more traditional fairy tales—kings and dwarfs, woodcutters and giants, magicians and talking animals—most of these stories are likely to depress young readers.

That Wilde was writing for an adult audience is also suggested by his prose style; it becomes increasingly ornate in *A House of Pomegranates*, making the stories, according to Yeats, "over decorated and seldom amusing."[2] Few children are likely to care that the young king admires an antique statue "inscribed with the name of the Bithynian slave of Hadrian," or that the throne room of the Spanish king includes "a black ebony cabinet, inlaid with plates of ivory, on which the figures from Holbein's Dance of Death had been graved." Indeed, even an adult audience may be forgiven for feeling that Wilde's lengthy descriptions of jewels, flowers, clothes, and furniture is sometimes a bit excessive.

Finally, the question of audience is raised by the humor of these stories, humor that is frequently satirical, especially when it comments on the manners and conventions of the society in which Wilde moved. In "The Devoted Friend," a duck counsels her children, "You will never be in the best society unless you can stand on your heads." When the swallow has an affair with a reed in "The Happy Prince," the other birds are indignant: "She has no money, and far too many relations; and indeed the river was quite full of Reeds." In "The Remarkable Rocket," a frog observes, "Arguments are extremely vulgar, for everybody in good society holds exactly the same opinions." And the rocket itself may be seen as a parody of the dandylike pose Wilde himself often affected. It complains that it finds itself living it a neighborhood that is "essentially suburban" and defends its lack of accomplishment on the grounds that "hard work is simply the refuge of people who have nothing to do." While not especially subtle, humor of this sort is still too complex to be readily understood by children.

When asked by a hostile reviewer if he considered *A House of Pomegranates* suitable for children, Wilde responded: "I had about as much intention of pleasing the British child as I had of pleasing the British public."[3] And this points to the chief problem with these stories. Too sophisticated for children and too contrived for adults, they suffer from an inadequately defined sense of audience. In expecting his tales to be both amusing and edifying, sensuously evocative and morally resolute, Wilde expected them to do too much. Had he made them either simpler or more consistently ironic, the result might have been more satisfying. But even if they do not reveal Wilde at his best, these stories should not be dismissed lightly. Offering much evidence of ethical concerns, they make it clear that Wilde was no simple decadent.

6

The Man of Sorrows:
De Profundis **and**
The Ballad of Reading Gaol

During the last six months of his imprisonment, Wilde composed a long letter to Lord Alfred Douglas in which he reviewed the history of their relations and chronicled the effect that prison had upon him. It is not known if this letter was ever delivered.[1] Upon his release from prison, Wilde gave the manuscript to Robert Ross with the instruction that several copies should be made. Ross eventually became Wilde's literary executor, and he published portions of this work in 1905, five years after Wilde's death. Ross deleted all references to Douglas and entitled the letter *De Profundis*, a title by which the work is still known, although Wilde himself had called it *Epistola: In Carcere et Vinculis*. The complete text was given to the British Museum on condition that it be kept sealed for fifty years.

An episode in autobiography, *De Profundis* never approaches the level of artistry which characterizes Wilde's work at its best. Its version of events is highly selective, and modern readers are apt to find it shrill and unconvincing. Nonetheless, it provides an unparalleled opportunity for seeing Wilde as he saw himself. For this reason, *De Profundis* remains among the most widely read of Wilde's works.

Wilde begins his epistle with an explanation of

why he was writing: "After long and fruitless waiting I have determined to write to you myself, as much for your sake as for mine, as I would not like to think that I had passed through two long years of imprisonment without ever having received a single line from you, or any news or message even, except such as gave me pain."[2] This statement reveals two of Wilde's motives; he writes to relieve himself of bitterness and to urge Douglas to reform his character. "I don't write this letter to put bitterness into your heart, but to pluck it out from mine." But he warns, "there will be much that will wound your vanity to the quick. If it prove so, read the letter over and over again till it kills your vanity."

As the letter takes shape, however, it becomes clear that Wilde is primarily interested in trying to justify himself before the world that had cast him out. He cannot bear to think that the "Gothic element in history" will cast him as a villain forevermore: "Your father will always live among the kind pure-minded parents of Sunday-school literature, your place is with the Infant Samuel, and in the lowest mire . . . I sit between Gilles de Retz and the Marquis de Sade." Wilde finds this ironic, since, in his view, he was the victim of a "fatal yielding" to a young man who held him completely in his power. He describes their relationship as "the triumph of the smaller over the bigger nature," and he utterly rejects the idea that he had corrupted Douglas: "Your defect was not that you knew so little about life, but that you knew so much."

But while Wilde complains of Douglas's fascination for the "gutter and the things that live in it," his principal complaint is that Douglas became a burden. Because he lacked "any power of sustained intellectual concentration," Douglas was never interested in working, and because of his "incapacity of being alone," he also kept Wilde from doing the work he might have

done. Wilde describes their friendship as "intellectually degrading to me." And he illustrates this claim by
describing a typical day:

I arrived at St. James's Place every morning at 11:30, in
order to have the opportunity of thinking and writing
without the interruptions inseparable from my own house-
hold . . . . But the attempt was vain. At twelve o'clock you
drove up, and stayed smoking cigarettes and chattering till
1:30, when I had to take you out to luncheon at the Café
Royal or the Berkeley. Luncheon with its liqueurs lasted
usually till 3:30. For an hour you retired to White's. At
tea-time you appeared again, and stayed till it was time to
dress for dinner. You dined with me either at the Savoy or
at Tite Street. We did not separate as a rule till after midnight, as supper at Willis's had to wind up the entrancing
day . . . it was a position at once grotesque and tragic.

Wilde also charges Douglas for having "demanded without grace and received without thanks."
With his insatiable appetite for luxurious living, Douglas brought Wilde "to utter and discreditable financial
ruin." Wilde devotes considerable space to detailing
the expenses he incurred on Douglas's behalf and
claims: "At the rate at which you wished to live, your
entire income for a whole year, if you had taken your
meals alone, had been especially economical in your
selection of the cheaper form of pleasures, would
hardly have lasted you three weeks." Later, when he
reflects upon his bankruptcy and the public auction of
his goods, Wilde complains that Douglas should have
purchased his library for him, "remembering the sums
of money I had lavishly spent on you and how you
had lived on me for years." More importantly, Douglas
should have paid Wilde's legal expenses:

You had taken personally on yourself the responsibility of
stating that your family would do so . . . . You were absolutely responsible. Even irrespective of your engagement
on your family's behalf you should have felt that as you had

brought the whole ruin on me, the least that you could have done was to spare me the additional ignominy of bankruptcy for an absolutely contemptible sum of money, less than half of what I spent on you in three brief months at Goring.

There is no question that Wilde was very generous to Douglas. But his claim that this generosity was never reciprocated is open to dispute. In his autobiography, Douglas argued that even before Wilde's bankruptcy, "I spent a great deal more money on Wilde than he spent on me."[3] And as for Wilde's claim that Douglas kept him from working, we have already seen that the record of Wilde's achievement suggests otherwise.[4]

Carried away with his own version of events, Wilde fails to explain adequately why he allowed such extravagance to continue. Casting himself as a victim, he is reluctant to concede that he might have chosen to stop paying for whatever Douglas desired. He tells us that at times he felt "almost polluted, as if by associating with one of such nature I had soiled and shamed my life irretrieveably," but nonetheless, he kept on paying the bills.

De Profundis is at its best when Wilde leaves complaint for analysis. Although he discusses at length "the terrible strain of your companionship," he also brings himself to admit to Douglas: "No matter what your conduct to me was I always felt that at heart you really did love me." And this goes far toward explaining why this fatally destructive friendship continued to stumble along. Whatever his exasperation with Douglas, he found it difficult to live without him.

In analyzing the events that brought him to prison, Wilde argues that his imprisonment had almost nothing to do with the evidence brought forth at his trials:

Do you think I am here on account of my relations with the witnesses at my trial? My relations, real or supposed, with people of that kind were matters of no interest to either the Government or Society. They knew nothing of them and cared less. I am here for having tried to put your father in prison.

Elsewhere he reflects:

Indeed my ruin came, not from too great individualism of life, but from too little. The one disgraceful, unpardonable, and to all time contemptible action of my life was my allowing myself to be forced into appealing to Society for help and protection from your father.

To ridicule convention and then bring a suit for libel was a betrayal of everything Wilde stood for, and he fully realized that he would never have gone to prison had he not done so.

Students of Wilde's life often wonder how he could have been so foolish as to sue the Marquess of Queensberry, knowing the sort of evidence that Queensberry could produce in support of his charge that Wilde posed as a sodomite. Wilde explains that he lost his head. Attacked by Queensberry on the one hand and goaded on by Lord Alfred Douglas on the other, Wilde claims that he did not know what he was doing:

My judgment forsook me. Terror took its place. I saw no possible escape, I may say frankly, from either of you. Blindly I staggered as an ox to the shambles. I had made a gigantic psychological error. I had always thought that my giving up to you in small things meant nothing: that when a great moment arrived I could reassert my will-power in its natural superiority. It was not so. At the great moment my will-power completely failed me. In life there is really no small or great thing . . . . My habit . . . of giving up to you in everything had become insensibly a real part of my nature.

In one of the most remarkable passages of *De Profundis*, Wilde explains why he was drawn to low company in the first place:

It was like feasting with panthers. The danger was half the excitement. I used to feel as the snake-charmer must feel when he lures the cobra to stir from the painted cloth or reed-basket that holds it, and makes it spread its hood at his bidding, and sway to and fro in the air as a plant sways restfully in a stream. They were to me the brightest of gilded snakes. Their poison was part of their perfection. I did not know that when they were to strike at me it was to be at your piping and for your father's pay.

Unrepentant, Wilde concludes by asserting, "I don't feel ashamed of having known them. They were intensely interesting."

As this passage suggests, Wilde was by no means crushed by the fate that had befallen him. Indeed, his ego seems to have been extraordinarily resilient. Wilde describes himself as "a man of world-wide reputation" —an exaggeration, surely, unless one defines "the world" to mean Britain, France, Germany, and America. He remembers "that beautiful unreal world of Art where once I was King" and boasts of his "great position" and "great name." He claims that his plays "beat Congreve for brilliancy . . . and I suppose everybody else for every other quality." If he admits that he is ashamed of his bankruptcy, it is not because of the creditors he had disappointed but because, as he puts it, "I was made for other things." Finally, his tribute to his own genius is not likely to convince the skeptical:

I was a man who stood in symbolic relations to the art and culture of my age. I had realized this for myself at the very dawn of my manhood, and had forced my age to realize it afterwards. Few men hold such a position in their own lifetime and have it so acknowledged . . . . Byron was a symbolic figure, but his relations were to the passion of

his age and its weariness of passion. Mine were to something more noble, more permanent, of more vital issue, of
larger scope.

The gods had given me everything. I had genius, a
distinguished name, high social position, brilliancy, intellectual daring: I made art a philosophy, and philosophy
an art: I altered the minds of men and the colours of
things: there was nothing I said or did that did not make
people wonder: I took the drama, the most objective form
known to art, and made it as personal a mode of expression as the lyric or the sonnet, at the same time that I
widened its range and enriched its characterization: drama,
novel, poem in rhyme, poem in prose, subtle or fantastic
dialogue, whatever I touched I made beautiful in a new
mode of beauty . . . . I awoke the imagination of my century
so that it created myth and legend around me: I summed
up all systems in a phrase, and all existence in an epigram.

It would be difficult to substantiate any of these
claims. Wilde has inflated his achievements, significant
though they were, far beyond their worth.

What is involved here, however, is a type of theater. Throughout *De Profundis*, Wilde casts himself as
the victim of a great tragedy. In order to impress his
readers (for he never intended this letter to be sent to
Lord Alfred Douglas alone) with the enormity of his
fall from grace, Wilde tries to establish himself as the
intellectual leader of an age that numbered, among his
contemporaries, Sigmund Freud, Thomas Hardy, Fred-
rich Nietzsche, William Butler Yeats, Richard Wag-
ner, and the French Impressionists. But this is not self-
delusion so much as self-dramatization. By the time of
his imprisonment, Wilde had come to look upon his
own life as a form of artistic expression, as if he were
forever a figure upon a public stage. In an illuminating
passage he observes:

I remember as I was sitting in the dock on the occasion of
my last trial listening to the prosecutor's appalling denunciation of me—like a thing out of Tacitus, like a passage

out of Dante, like one of Savonarola's indictments of the Popes at Rome—and being sickened with horror at what I heard. Suddenly it occurred to me, "*How splendid it would be, if I was saying all this about myself!*"[5]

Nothing appeals to him so much as the dramatic; he would play any role if the lines were memorable. It is important to read *De Profundis* with this understanding in mind: Wilde is often less interested in telling the truth—elusive though that may be—than he is in making a great impression.

This tendency toward the theatrical leads Wilde, on occasion, into obvious insincerity, as when he declares, "I have no desire to complain." Equally unconvincing is his claim that although he is "completely penniless and absolutely homeless"—an exaggeration in itself—he would "gladly and readily beg his bread from door to door" if he were only able to leave prison without bitterness in his heart. And the history of his final years does not support his professed conversion to the simple life: "If after I go out a friend of mine gave a feast, and did not invite me to it, I shouldn't mind a bit. I can be perfectly happy by myself. With freedom, books, flowers, and the moon, who would not be happy?" Wilde himself may have believed these lines as he wrote them, but the role he assumes here was cast off at sight of the first café.

Similarly, there is something false about Wilde's claim that prison has improved his character. He tells us that he wants "to get to the point when I shall be able to say, quite simply and without affectation, that the two great turning-points of my life were when my father sent me to Oxford, and when society sent me to prison." Already he feels that he is "a *deeper* man," for this "is the privilege of those who have suffered." Having overcome "the bitterness of lonely exile," he is now in harmony with "the great heart of the world"— or so he would have us believe.

But Wilde no sooner proclaims himself a nobler man than he slips into language that is brutally vindictive. He compares Douglas's letters to "the froth and foam of an epileptic," for example. And his portrait of the Marquess of Queensberry, with his "apelike face," could not have come from a man at peace with himself: "I used to see your father bustling in and out of court in the hopes of attracting public attention, as if anyone could fail to note or remember the stableman's gait and dress, the bowed legs, the twitching hands, the hanging lower lip, the bestial and half-witted grin."

But the most significant insincerity within *De Profundis* is that Wilde declares on page after page that he had tried in vain to end his friendship with Douglas at the same time he is complaining that Douglas is no longer corresponding with him. If his disgust with Douglas was as genuine as Wilde would have us think, then he should have been relieved that their friendship had apparently come to an end. There is a distinct lack of candor in Wilde's account of his own feelings. He was still very much attached to Douglas and went to live with him in Naples shortly after his release from prison. If Wilde had been willing to explore the full range of his feeling for Douglas, he might have produced, in this letter, a richer work of art. As it is, he too often allows the work to degenerate to the level of an epistolary lover's quarrel.

It would be easier to excuse the emotional excesses of *De Profundis* if we could believe that it came pouring from Wilde's heart without thought as he sat alone in his prison cell. But Wilde himself makes it clear that the letter is carefully edited. He tells Douglas:

You must take it as it stands . . . and make it out as best as you can, blots, corrections and all. As for the corrections and *errata*, I have made them in order that my words should be an absolute expression of my thoughts, and err neither through surplusage nor through being inadequate . . . . As it stands, at any rate, my letter has its definite meaning behind every phrase. There is in it nothing of rhetoric.

It almost seems as if Wilde had learned nothing from prison. "For prison-life, with its endless privations and restrictions, makes one rebellious. The most terrible thing about it is not that it breaks one's heart . . . but that it turns one's heart to stone." Whatever his suffering—and it was severe—Wilde's pride remained intact and his obsession with Lord Alfred Douglas undiminished. And when in the second half of *De Profundis* Wilde turns his attention to explaining his philosophy of life, it soon becomes evident that his values remain essentially the same.

Wilde tells us that it would be "fatal" for him to forget, after his release, that he had been imprisoned. "To reject one's own experiences is to arrest one's own development." But this is the very doctrine that Wilde had learned from Walter Pater at Oxford twenty years earlier. This cult of experience enables Wilde to believe, or at least to argue, that he is living in the best of all possible worlds.

I don't regret for a single moment having lived for pleasure. I did it to the full, as one should do everything to the full. There was no pleasure I did not experience . . . . But to have continued the same life would have been wrong because it would have been limiting. I had to pass on.

Now, he declares, he has discovered suffering. Observing that "there is about Sorrow an intense, an extraordinary reality," Wilde seems to relish his ordeal, like a Dorian Gray who has discovered a new thrill. According to Wilde, sorrow is "the supreme emotion of which man is capable," the ultimate high, as it were:

It is really a revelation. One discerns things that one never discerned before. One approaches the whole of history from a different standpoint. What one had felt dimly through instinct, about Art, is intellectually and emotionally realized with perfect clearness of vision and absolute intensity of apprehension.

But Wilde contradicts himself. While proclaiming that he has acquired "a different standpoint" that came to him as "a revelation," he ends by declaring that he was right all along—what he had previously felt through instinct is now clearly vindicated for him. His "standpoint" is thus indistinguishable from his earlier point of view; the only difference is that he now holds his beliefs more strongly than ever.

Wilde argues: "The supreme vice is shallowness. Everything that is realized is right." And he frequently repeats this assertion throughout the text, as a sort of refrain designed to give it a degree of unity. The nature of one's experience is less important than the way one responds to and profits from one's experience. "But while I see that there is nothing wrong in what one does, I see that there is something wrong in what one becomes." Self-realization is the ultimate goal in life.

Even when Wilde discusses his newly acquired admiration for Christ—which he does at considerable length—it is evident that his values have remained unchanged; he has simply transposed them to another key. His version of the Savior is unlike any other. He describes Christ as "the true precursor of the romantic movement in life" and declares that "the very basis of his nature was the same as that of the nature of the artist, an intense and flamelike imagination." This Christ has been stripped of his divinity. His place "is with the poets . . . he wakes in us that temper of wonder to which Romance always appeals." He owes this appeal to "the charm of his personality," and he becomes, in Wilde's view, "the most supreme of Individualists." He becomes for Wilde the source of all beautiful art: the artist as Son of God. We owe to this "fascinating personality" "Hugo's *Les Miserables*, Baudelaire's *Fleurs du Mal*, the note of pity in Russian novels, the stained glass and tapestries . . . of Burne-Jones and Morris, Lancelot and Guinevere, Tannhauser, the troubled romantic marbles of Michael Angelo, pointed architecture, and the love of children and flowers." It would seem then that Christ was an artist and a gentleman, a sort of early Oscar Wilde.

Similarly, when Wilde speaks of his love of the Gospels, he might easily be speaking of the work of some neglected poet. Reporting that reading a dozen verses is "a delightful way of opening the day," Wilde praises "the freshness, the simple romantic charm of the Gospels." Their appeal is primarily aesthetic. So far from being a penitent who has been born again, Wilde remains the connoisseur who savors the New Testament, but only as a suggestive work of literature, an elaborate prose poem.

A careful reading of *De Profundis* thus reveals that Wilde cannot always be taken at his word. He claims to have undergone a greater metamorphosis in character and belief than is, in fact, the case. He is neither so humble nor so forgiving as he affects. And whatever his fascination with the person of Christ, Wilde remains the artist at odds with social norms, "one of those who are made for exceptions, not for laws."

But it does not necessarily follow that Wilde was hypocritical. If *De Profundis* suffers from too many changes in mood, changes that seem to border, at times, on outright contradiction, it is because Wilde was at odds with himself. He realized this himself, and in his conclusion reflects: "How far I am away from the true temper of soul, this letter in its changing, uncertain moods, its scorn and bitterness, its aspirations and its failure to reach those aspirations, shows you quite clearly." Uneven and unconvincing, *De Profundis* nonetheless offers numerous insights into the conflicts which drove Wilde to the abyss.

During the months that immediately followed his release from prison, Wilde wrote a long poem, *The Ballad of Reading Gaol*. When it was first published, in February 1898, Wilde's name was not used; the author was cited simply as C.3.3., Wilde's identification number in prison. It was widely recognized that Wilde was the author, however, and although it received almost no advertising, the poem went through six editions within three months of its release. Part of its success was due, no doubt, to curiosity—here was the public's first chance to learn how prison had affected Wilde. But *The Ballad of Reading Gaol* can easily stand on its own merits; it is unquestionably the best poetry Wilde ever wrote.

Subdivided into six sections composed of varying numbers of sestets, 109 altogether, the poem tells the story of one of Wilde's fellow prisoners, a young soldier who was hung for having murdered his wife. It begins with the man's arrival at the prison and follows him through the three weeks he spent there, chronicling his execution and the effect it had upon the other prisoners.

Wilde tells us that sympathy for what this man had to endure caused him to forget his own problems.

> I walked, with other souls in pain,
>   Within another ring,
> And was wondering if the man had done
>   A great or little thing,
> When a voice behind me whispered low,
>   *'That fellow's got to swing.'*
>
> Dear Christ! the very prison walls
>   Suddenly seemed to reel,

> And the sky above my head became
>   Like a casque of scorching steel;
> And, though I was a soul in pain,
>   My pain I could not feel.

This may account for the impact the poem has upon those who read it. Whereas Wilde had dwelled on his own experience in *De Profundis*, sometimes falling victim to self-pity in the process, in *The Ballad of Reading Gaol* he subordinates that experience to the experience of another. No longer the center of attention, Wilde avoids the mawkishness that was apt to emerge when he reflected upon his own injuries. Imaginatively engaged by the story of someone who suffered more than he did himself, Wilde is able to tell that story with remarkable power.

The soldier who inspired the poem had cut his wife's throat. Wilde does not defend him for having done so, but he argues that there are worse ways to kill the things we love. Moreover, the murderer should not be seen as exceptional; everyone is ultimately guilty of the same crime.

> Yet each man kills the thing he loves,
>   By each let this be heard,
> Some do it with a bitter look,
>   Some with a flattering word,
> The coward does it with a kiss,
>   The brave man with a sword!
>
> Some kill their love when they are young,
>   And some when they are old;
> Some strangle with the hands of Lust,
>   Some use the hands of Gold:
> The kindest use a knife, because
>   The dead so soon grow cold.
>
> Some love too little, some too long,
>   Some sell, and others buy;
> Some do the deed with many tears,

> And some without a sigh:
> For each man kills the thing he loves
> Yet each man does not die.

To kill the thing one loves is the worst of all possible sins, and we are all guilty of precisely this sin. Wilde does not mean to excuse the soldier but to teach us that we share his guilt. It is a way of engaging our sympathy for his subject.

Wilde increases this sympathy by emphasizing the terrible condition of life in a nineteenth-century prison:

> Each narrow cell in which we dwell
> Is a foul and dark latrine,
> And the fetid breath of living Death
> Chokes up each grated screen,
> And all, but Lust, is turned to dust
> In Humanity's Machine.

Drawing upon incidents that he himself had witnessed, Wilde charges that the warders are deliberately brutal:

> For they starve the little frightened child
> Till it weeps both night and day:
> And they scourge the weak, and flog the fool,
> And gibe the old and grey,
> And some grow mad, and all grow bad,
> And none a word may say.[6]

Such prisons represent the complete denial of Christianity:

> This too I know—and wise it were
> If each could know the same—
> That every prison that men build
> Is built with bricks of shame,
> And bound with bars lest Christ should see
> How men their brothers maim.

Christ is a regular presence throughout the poem, and He is specifically associated with the young soldier with whom Wilde would have us sympathize. The chaplain who escorts the soldier to his execution is compared to Caiaphas, the priest who condemned Christ. Like Christ, who demanded why His father had forsaken Him, the condemned man cries out bitterly before he dies, but only once. When Wilde subsequently imagines him covered with "bloody sweat," the image is more appropriate to one who is stretched, crucified, in the Middle Eastern sun than to a convict hung quickly at an English dawn. And like Christ, the murderer is mocked by those who kill him:

> They stripped him of his canvas clothes,
>   And gave him to the flies:
> They mocked the swollen purple throat,
>   And the stark and staring eyes:
> And with laughter loud they heaped the shroud
>   In which the convict lies.

After the victim is thrown into an unmarked grave,

> The Chaplain would not kneel to pray
>   By his dishonoured grave:
> Nor mark it with that blessed Cross
>   That Christ for sinners gave,
> Because the man was one of those
>   Whom Christ came down to save.

Through the chaplain, Wilde is criticizing the Church for cooperating with an unjust and brutal system. He is part of an unfeeling triumvirate that rules the prison with mechanical efficiency:

> The Governor was strong upon
>   The Regulations Act:
> The Doctor said that Death was but
>   A scientific fact:
> And twice a day the Chaplain called,
>   And left a little tract.

This is almost caricature. But it is part of Wilde's extended attack on modern justice. There is no resisting "Humanity's machine"; it indiscriminately destroys everything in its path.

> For Man's grim Justice goes its way,
>> And will not swerve aside:
> It slays the weak, it slays the strong,
>> It has a deadly stride.

In opposition to the prison, Wilde sets the world of nature, representing freedom, beauty, and growth. The prisoners relish the sight of the sky during their daily exercise period, a sky that Wilde describes as a "tent of blue"—a phrase that suggests the reality of his own life behind walls. The condemned man is especially grateful for contact with nature:

> He did not wring his hands nor weep,
>> Nor did he peek or pine,
> But he drank the air as though it held
>> Some healthful anondyne;
> With open mouth he drank the sun
>> As though it had been wine!

Later, after the soldier has been killed and buried, Wilde imagines how "God's kindly earth" might yield beautiful flowers upon the grave, symbolizing the forgiveness of Christ. But prison policy is designed to keep men in despair, and the grave is left barren:

> The shard, the pebble, and the flint,
>> Are what they give us there:
> For flowers have been known to heal
>> A common man's despair.

Only ugliness flourishes in "the iron town":

> The vilest deeds like poison weeds
>> Bloom well in prison-air;
> It is only what is good in Man
>> That wastes and withers there . . .

But Wilde provides a consolation before the poem ends. Returning to an idea he had advanced in "The Fisherman and His Soul," Wilde argues that intense suffering prepares the soul for redemption. The brutality of prison life is "heart-breaking," but a broken heart is preferable to a heart turned to stone:

> Ah! happy they whose hearts can break
>   And peace of pardon win!
> How else may man make straight his plan
>   And cleanse his soul from Sin?
> How else but through a broken heart
>   May Lord Christ enter in?

Because the soldier had "a broken and a contrite heart," he is saved, like the thief whom Christ took to paradise. Of all the prisoners, he alone sleeps peacefully on the eve of his execution. And after he dies, "he has but passed," leaving "the Secret House of Shame" for "the seat of grace." Wilde assures us that "all is well"; in so doing, he encourages us to transfer our sympathy from the soldier to the prisoners left behind. For the other men in the prison, there is no release.

Wilde does not try to ennoble the prisoners; on the contrary, he takes pains to make them grotesque. "Like ape or clown in monstrous garb," with "shaven head and feet of lead," they are "mad mourners," and "a merry masquerade"—merry only in the sense that there is something comic about freaks. Such images contribute to Wilde's argument that prison is degrading. We sympathize with "the fool, the fraud, the knave" because we are led to see them as victims of a cruel system. Deliberately stripped of all dignity, the prisoners nonetheless earn our respect by virtue of what they endure.

> We tore the tarry rope to shreds,
>   With blunt and bleeding nails:
> We rubbed the doors, and scrubbed the floors,

> And cleaned the shining rails:
> And rank by rank, we soaped the plank,
>   And clattered with the pails.
>
> We sewed the sacks, we broke the stones,
>   We turned the dusty drill:
> We banged the tins, and bawled the hymns,
>   And sweated on the mill . . .

As these lines suggest, Wilde's diction throughout the poem is stark and simple. He favors words of one or two syllables that reflect the desolation of prison life. Such words as "tore," "rope," "blunt," "nails," "rank," and "tins" convey through their sound alone the harshness of prison life. Gone, for the most part, is the elaborate Latinate language that characterizes so much of Wilde's earlier work. And when Wilde does use words like "arabesques" or "pirouettes," it is only to describe the evil visions that keep the prisoners from sleeping on the eve of the execution—a seven stanza lapse that the poem could easily spare.

In keeping with his determination to portray the barrenness of Reading Gaol, Wilde emphasizes the absence of color. The first line of the poem tells us that the murderer "did not wear his scarlet coat" when he arrived in prison but "a suit of shabby gray." The chaplain is "robed in white," the governor all in "shiny black." When the prisoners kneel down to pray for the condemned man's soul, they are "grey figures on the floor." A "grey cock" crows at dawn. And reminded of their own mortality, "this man's face was white with fear / And that man's face was gray."

The introduction of more vivid color comes midway through the poem, but it is associated with suffering rather than beauty. The open grave that awaits the murderer is described as "the yellow hole," and there are two references to the "swollen purple throat" of the corpse. On the morning of the execution "God's dreadful dawn was red," and elsewhere Wilde writes of the "red Hell" to which our souls may stray. It is true that the beauty of color is momentarily evoked when Wilde envisions the red and white roses that might remind the prisoners "that God's Son died for all." But this is a vision only: "Neither milk-white rose nor red / May bloom in prison air." And if the sky is blue early in the poem, the prisoners are allowed only a brief glimpse of it before it becomes "leaden."

The consistency of Wilde's diction and imagery contributes to the unity of the poem, a unity that is further strengthened through the effective use of binding repetition. Woven throughout the poem, lines like "each man kills the thing he loves" serve as a refrain, helping to hold the poem together while emphasizing its principal themes. *The Ballad of Reading Gaol* thus achieves that sense of the inevitable that characterizes great art. We find here none of the conflicts that make so many of Wilde's works seemingly at odds with themselves. As a result, the poem has a directness that conveys the reality of suffering far more powerfully than the detailed complaints and catalogued regrets of *De Profundis*.

7

The Dialectic of a Dandy: What Wilde Believed

Having completed our survey of Wilde's principal works, it would be useful to step back and consider them within the context of the critical essays he wrote in the eighties and early nineties. For in addition to being a novelist, playwright, and poet, Wilde was also a critic, and his contributions to criticism are by no means negligible. Moreover, an understanding of Wilde's criticism adds significantly to our understanding of his work as a whole.

Wilde supported himself as a critic for over five years, churning out anonymous book reviews for *The Pall Mall Gazette*.[1] Then there are the lectures through which he first established himself as a public figure, the two most important of which are "The English Renaissance of Art" and "House Decoration." *Intentions*, a collection of four essays published in 1891, includes "The Decay of Lying," "Pen Pencil and Poison," "The Critic as Artist," and "The Truth in Masks." "The Soul of Man under Socialism," Wilde's best-known essay, also dates from 1891, although it was privately printed as a small book in 1895. All of these essays represent an attempt to define the nature of art, the function of criticism, and the role of the artist in society. They overlap and sometimes seem to contradict one another. But they are invariably provocative and help to reveal what Wilde believed—a philosophy of art and life that we must understand before passing final judgment upon him.

Wilde is seldom remembered as a social thinker. Indeed, he often sounds supremely indifferent to consideration of social ills. In *The Picture of Dorian Gray*, Lord Henry Wotton declares, "The nineteenth century has gone bankrupt through the over-expenditure of sympathy." Sympathy for the poor is described as "the special vice of the age" in *A Woman of No Importance*. And when Lord Caversham, in *An Ideal Husband*, complains that there is a great deal too much sympathy "going around today," Lord Goring responds: "I quite agree with your father. If there was less sympathy in the world there would be less trouble in the world." Such lines as these sound heartless and glib.

But we know from *The Happy Prince* that Wilde did have sympathy for the poor. The object of his scorn was never poverty but cant. In "The Critic as Artist" Wilde observed: "It is so easy for people to have sympathy with suffering." He recognized that it costs us little so long as we ourselves are in a comfortably superior position. Rather than "sympathize" with the poor, we should restructure society so that the poor no longer need our sympathy because they are no longer poor. Wilde develops this idea in "The Soul of Man under Socialism."

According to Wilde, "charity degrades and demoralizes." Altruism is "sentimental": when liberals go to work in slums, "their remedies do not cure the disease: they merely prolong it. Indeed, their remedies are part of the disease." Poverty is really a form of slavery. And "just as the worst slave-owners were those who were kind to their slaves, and so prevented the horror of the system being realized," modern philanthropists perpetuate social evils by making them

bearable by those who should, by rights, rebel against
them.

Wilde argues that "the best amongst the poor are
never grateful" and that the so-called virtuous poor
deserve pity, perhaps, but not admiration: "They have
made private terms with the enemy, and sold their
birthright for very bad pottage. They must be extraordinarily stupid." The more intelligent and enter-
prising among the poor realize they are victimized by
an unjust system; they are not likely to be satisfied
with "a sentimental dole, usually accompanied by
some impertinent attempt to tyrannize over their private lives." He asks, "Why should they be grateful for
the crumbs that fall from the rich man's table?" Thus
when Mabel Chiltern, in *An Ideal Husband*, tells us
that she works for "an excellent charity: in aid of the
Undeserving, the only people I am really interested
in," the line, in retrospect, is something more than
funny.

Since capitalism is intrinsically unfair, Wilde ad-
vocates socialism, but a socialism unlike any the world
has yet to see enacted. He stands completely opposed
to what he calls "Authoritarian Socialism," arguing
that in "an industrial-barrack system, or a system of
economic tyranny, nobody would have any freedom at
all." Compulsion of any sort is out of the question.
Without granting "economic power" to the state—for
that would lead to "Industrial Tyranny"—Wilde envisions government as "a voluntary association that will
organize labour, and be the manufacturer and distrib-
utor of necessary commodities."

Wilde is hopelessly vague about how such a state
would be organized or how it might be brought about.
And in arguing that authority would not be necessary
in a justly organized society, he sounds naïve, to say
the least. He seems to believe that human nature is
infinitely perfectible and evil merely the result of a
poor environment.[2] At times he even seems to be an

anarchist. "All authority is quite degrading," he tells us, "it degrades those who exercise it, and degrades those over whom it is exercised."

This contempt for authority led Wilde to become fascinated with criminals—an interest he shared with other late nineteenth-century Romantics:

A man cannot always be estimated by what he does. He may keep the law, and yet be worthless . . . . He may commit a sin against society, and yet realize through that sin his true perfection.

This is an idea to which Wilde would return in other works. In "The Critic as Artist," he declares that "there is no sin except stupidity":

To be good, according to the vulgar standard of goodness, is obviously quite easy. It merely requires a certain amount of sordid terror, a certain low passion for middle-class respectability.

And in "Pen Pencil and Poison," Wilde devotes an entire essay to defending Thomas Griffins Waine-wright, a respected art critic who became "a forger of no mean or ordinary capabilities . . . a subtle and secret poisoner almost without rival in this or any age." According to Wilde, "the fact of a man being a poisoner is nothing against his prose." Lord Henry Wotton would have agreed. In *The Picture of Dorian Gray*, he defined crime as "a method of procuring extraordinary sensations" and sin as "the only real color-element in modern life."

At least part of Wilde's fascination with crime can be traced to the fact that it is so much more interesting than work—it is an act of rebellion against the tendency of the age to treat human beings as automatons. Throughout the nineteenth century, social philosophers had celebrated the dignity of labor, but Wilde disagreed:

There is nothing necessarily dignified about manual labour at all, and most of it is absolutely degrading. . . . To

sweep a slushy crossing for eight hours a day when the
east wind is blowing is a disgusting occupation. To sweep
it with joy would be appalling. Man is made for something
better than disturbing dirt.

Such work is brutalizing. And Wilde realized that
nothing in which he believed—be it beauty, art, or
scholarship—was possible so long as men and women
were condemned to work of this sort.

Wilde therefore became an advocate of the machine, believing that machinery must do "anything
that is tedious and distressing." Unfortunately, "as
soon as man had invented the machine to do his work
he began to starve." This is the result, however, of
private property—the machine itself is not to blame.
Under capitalism, one man owns a machine that can
do the work of five hundred; those workers are conse-
quently left unemployed, and the owner of the
machine "has five hundred times as much as he should
have." It is this logic that led Wilde to plead for socialism. If publicly owned and operated for the common
good, machinery will free men and women from "ugly,
horrible, uninteresting work."

Wilde's ultimate interests, however, are neither
political nor economic. The principle benefit of socialism is that "it will lead to Individualism." With its
emphasis on private property, capitalism discourages
culture "by confusing a man with what he possesses."
As a result, "man thought that the important thing was
to have, and did not know that the important thing is
to be." If society were reconstructed so that it became
impossible for human beings to be "compelled to do
the work of beasts of burden" at one extreme, or to
squander their lives "wearily and tediously" accu-
mulating great fortunes at the other, then the arts
would flourish as never before.

Wilde believed not only that "behind everything wonderful stands the individual," but that ultimately "Art

is Individualism." Because it stands apart from commonly accepted values, art is "a disturbing and disintegrating force" that can undermine the rule of authority. The public therefore fears art and tries to control it:

In Art, the public accept what has been, because they cannot alter it, not because they appreciate it. They swallow their classics whole, and never taste them . . . . The fact is, the public makes use of the classics of a country as a means of checking the progress of Art. They degrade the classics into authorities. They use them as bludgeons for preventing the free expression of Beauty in new forms. They are always asking a writer why he does not write like somebody else, or a painter why he does not paint like somebody else, quite oblivious of the fact that if either of them did anything of the kind he would cease to be an artist.

To attempt to control or censor art is to stifle the life of the mind. As Algernon observes in *The Importance of Being Earnest*: "It is absurd to have hard-and-fast rules about what one should read and what one shouldn't. More than half of modern culture depends upon what one shouldn't read."

Wilde's plea for artistic freedom springs from the fact that he himself was in direct opposition to the prevailing aesthetic of his age, what Ruskin called "the Naturalist Ideal." The attempt to capture on canvas the beauty of nature characterizes major works of art from the end of the eighteenth century to the beginning of the twentieth. But the naturalist ideal also inspired countless paintings that never rise above the level of those predictably lovely landscapes that decorate so many calendars.

If nineteenth-century academicians sought to capture the beauty of nature through the painstaking portrayal of almost photographic detail, the literature of the period was motivated by a similar impulse. The subject was usually different from that of painting—

Dickens had discovered the slums, and throughout the second half of the last century a growing number of writers sought to capture reality by delineating those aspects of life that had previously been considered too sordid for fiction. But the method of realism is essentially one and the same with the method of those academic painters who so carefully tried to reproduce exactly what they saw. In both cases, art sought to imitate life. And nearly all of Wilde's work is aimed at the futility of this attempt.

Nature had no charm for Wilde. He criticized its "lack of design, her curious crudities, her extraordinary monotony, her absolutely unfinished condition." In his view, "Art is our spirited protest, our gallant attempt to teach Nature her proper place." He humorously complained: "Nature is so uncomfortable. Grass is hard and lumpy and damp and full of black insects . . . . If Nature had been comfortable, mankind would never have invented architecture." Architecture is superior to Nature because within a beautifully designed building, "everything is subordinated to us." In short, art imposes order upon chaos; it is more beautiful than nature because it is shaped and refined.

In literature, as in art, one must create "from the rough material of actual existence, a new world that will be more marvelous, more enduring, and more true than the world that common eyes look upon." It is essential to avoid direct imitation; great works are inevitably artificial. "To be natural is to be obvious, and to be obvious is to be inartistic." Declaring that there is "an absolute difference between the world of art and the world of real fact," Wilde was led to dismiss realism as "a complete failure." Arguing that we require in literature "distinction, charm, and imaginative power," he complained of those novelists who "find life crude, and leave it raw." It therefore follows that "wherever we have returned to Life and Nature, our work has always become vulgar, common, and uninteresting."

At this point, the principal weakness of Wilde's position begins to become clear. Demanding complete autonomy for the arts, Wilde nevertheless proceeded to define art in such a way as to limit both its subject and its method. Believing that great art gives us a sense of "calm and perfect repose," he argued that "into the secure and sacred house of Beauty the true artist will admit nothing that is harsh and disturbing, nothing that gives us pain, nothing that is debatable, nothing about which men argue." The irony is that this rebel against authority is echoing the supreme authority of an earlier era—Matthew Arnold, the great Victorian critic, who had told the generation previous to Wilde's that

any accurate representation may . . . be expected to be interesting; but if the representation be a poetical one, more than this is demanded. It is demanded, not only that it shall interest, but also that it shall inspirit and rejoice the reader: that it convey a charm, and infuse delight . . . it is not enough that the Poet should add to the knowledge of men, it is required of him also that he should add to their happiness.[3]

The irony is compounded when we realize that, in this respect, Wilde was seldom faithful to his own aesthetic. In *The Picture of Dorian Gray*, for example, there is much that is "disturbing" and "debatable." And we have seen how the same can be said of even such seemingly frivolous works as *The Importance of Being Earnest*.

But Wilde was clever enough to provide his own defense. Aware that he occasionally contradicted himself, he argued, in "The Critic as Artist" that the true critic

will never suffer himself to be limited to any settled custom of thought, or stereotyped mode of looking at things. He will realize himself in many forms, and by a thousand different ways, and will ever be curious of new sensations and fresh points of view. Through constant change, and constant change alone, he will find his true unity. He will not consent to be the slave of his own opinions.

If we approach Wilde's philosophy as something fluid rather than fixed—something in the process of becoming—what appear to be contradictions can be understood to represent different stages in his development.

In *The Picture of Dorian Gray,* Lord Henry Wotton had argued that "art has no influence upon action. It annihilates the desire to act. It is superbly sterile." And during the course of Wilde's relatively short career, he came to place less and less emphasis upon the content of a work of art, valuing instead its form. How something was said ultimately mattered more to him than what was being said. In "The English Renaissance of Art," he had warned his audiences:

It is not an increased moral sense, an increased moral supervision that your literature needs. Indeed, one should never talk of a moral or an immoral poem—poems are either well written or badly written, that is all.

Ten years later, he returned to this idea in his preface to *The Picture of Dorian Gray*: "There is no such thing as a moral or an immoral book. Books are well written, or badly written. That is all." Wilde believed that art could inspire us to action; the basic theme of "The Decay of Lying" is that "life imitates Art."[4] But he felt that artists have no real obligations outside of their art. "No artist tries to prove anything." A work of art may be profoundly moral, but only as a side-effect. The moment an artist sets out to be didactic, the work becomes stilted and incomplete. As Gwendolen Fairfax puts it in *The Importance of Being Earnest,* "Style, not sincerity is the vital thing."

This aspect of Wilde's thought is distinctly modern. In criticizing painting, Wilde came to single out "colour and design" as the two most important attributes of art:

Mere colour, unspoiled by meaning, and unallied with definite form, can speak to the soul in a thousand different ways. The harmony that resides in the delicate proportions of lines and masses becomes mirrored in the mind. The repetitions of pattern give us rest. The marvels of design stir the imagination.

He might well be anticipating Mondrian. Applied to literature, this aesthetic led Wilde to emphasize the sound of language rather than its sense. As early as 1881 he praised Rossetti for a style characterized by "a sustaining consciousness of the musical value of each word as opposed to that value which is merely intellectual." Even prose should be "a passage of music" revealing "the rhythmical life of words and the fine freedom and richness of effect that such rhythmical life produces." Elsewhere he complained of the tendency of modern literature "to appeal more and more to the eye, and less and less to the ear which is really the sense which, from the standpoint of pure art, it should seek to please." Thus, when Algernon Moncrieff tells Jack Worthing in *The Importance of Being Earnest* that it does not matter if an observation is true so long as it is "perfectly phrased," he is not being glib; on the contrary, he is advancing a philosophy that Wilde had been arguing for at least ten years. Debatable though it may be, it deserves to be taken seriously.

Wilde realized that "the perfectly phrased" does not come easily, and he emphasized that art requires discipline. "All fine imaginative work is self-conscious and deliberate. No poet sings because he must sing. At least, no great poet does. A great poet sings because he chooses to sing." Therefore, great art has "definite conception" and "clearness of vision." The Romantic poets had rebelled against reason, but it does not follow that artists need do nothing but open up their hearts. Wilde cautioned against the celebration of "feeling" as a good in itself, arguing that "in this century it is rather against the claims of the emotional faculties, the claims of mere sentiment and feeling, that the artist must react." He singled out Keats as the greatest of the Romantics and praised him for "the calmness and clearness of his vision, his perfect self-control, his unerring sense of beauty and his recognition of a separate realm for the imagination."

However difficult it may be to achieve such art, it is worth the effort, "for beauty is the only thing that time cannot harm. Philosophies fall away like sand, and creeds follow one another like the withered leaves of autumn; but what is beautiful is a joy for all seasons and a possession for all eternity."

Recognizing as he did the difficulties that confront the artist, Wilde argued on behalf of criticism as an important aspect of the arts. He warned that "if the passion for creation be not accompanied by the critical, the aesthetic faculty also, it will be sure to waste its strength aimlessly." Indeed, he believed that the antithesis of creativity and criticism is "entirely arbitrary." Properly understood, the two are really one and the same.

Criticism is itself an art. And just as artistic creation implies the working of the critical faculty, and indeed without it cannot be said to exist at all, so Criticism is really creative in the highest sense of the word.

Art would stagnate without criticism, since "the tendency of creation is to repeat itself." Because it continually demands new forms, criticism might be described as the most creative of the arts:

> It is very much more difficult to talk about a thing than to do it . . . . Anybody can make history. Only a great man can write it. There is no mode of action, no form of emotion, that we do not share with the lower animals. It is only by language that we rise above them, or above each other—by language, which is the parent, and not the child of thought.

In keeping with his belief that criticism is "creative," Wilde advocated a form of criticism that is frankly subjective. "To the critic the work of art is simply a suggestion for a new work of his own, that need not necessarily bear any obvious resemblance to the thing it criticizes." Accordingly, "the highest criticism really is the record of one's own soul."

Whereas "objective criticism" seeks to reduce each work to a fixed understanding of what it is in itself—"to see the object as in itself it really is"—"subjective criticism" has the advantage of encouraging the infinite multiplication of artistic impressions. In the modern world, "we have so few mysteries left to us that we cannot afford to part with any of them." Therefore, it is the role of criticism to expose the mystery that great works of art embody, without "trying to explain their divinity away."

The critic proceeds by recognizing that there is no one meaning inherent in any great work of art; its meaning—or, more accurately, meanings—derives only from the impressions it inspires. Critics therefore freely record their own impressions, describing not the work itself but what they see in it—an important distinction. Such criticism "does not confine itself . . . to discovering the real intention of the artist and accepting that as final." Wilde is eventually led to conclude that the critic's aim is "to see the object as it

really is not"—a deliberate inversion of Arnold's famous dictum and a sharp break with a method of
criticism that lasted well into the twentieth century.

Wilde's advocacy of subjective criticism springs in
part from his fascination with individualism. He believed that a healthy society is one in which men and
women are able to achieve maximum self-development
independent of external pressure to conform to any
fixed standard. His theory of literary and artistic criticism is the logical extension of the political views he
had advanced in "The Soul of Man under Socialism."
Ultimately, Wilde is more interested in the audience
than in the art; art is only a means toward self-development.

This leads to another contradiction within Wilde's
philosophy. In arguing for artistic freedom, Wilde
wrote in "The Soul of Man" that:

the work of art is to dominate the spectator: the spectator
is not to dominate the work of art. The spectator is to be
receptive. He is to be the violin on which the master is to
play. And the more completely he can surpress his own
silly views, his own foolish prejudices, his own absurd
ideas of what Art should be or not be, the more likely he
is to understand and appreciate the work of art in question.

But in "The Critic as Artist," Wilde not only argued
that the sole aim of the critic is "to chronicle his own
impressions," he even claimed that the critic should
have "preferences": "It is only an auctioneer who can
equally and impartially admire all schools of Art."

This apparent contradiction is partially resolved,
however, by the distinction Wilde makes between "the
suburban intellect" and "the true critic." A work of art
may inspire an infinite number of interpretations, but
it does not follow that all of these interpretations are
of equal value. Some are the product of "silly views
and foolish prejudices," and they should not be taken

seriously. But others come to us from "a temperament exquisitely susceptible to beauty" and a mind to which "no form of thought is alien, no emotional impulse obscure."

In 1881, Wilde defined the artist as one to whom "the present will not be . . . a whit more real than the past; for . . . the poet is the spectator of all time and all existence. For him no form is obsolete, no subject out of date." Ten years later, he extended this definition to include the critic. Arguing that the true critic is "he who bears within himself the dreams, and ideas, and feelings of myriad generations," Wilde concluded:

For he to whom the present is the only thing that is present, knows nothing of the age in which he lives. To realize the nineteenth century, one must realize every century that has preceded it and that has contributed to its making. To know anything about oneself, one must know all about others.

The true critic is well-educated. But Wilde also believed that "nothing that is worth knowing can be taught." Thus the true critic does not simply have a university degree but can also comprehend knowledge through the gifts of temperament and imagination.

The exercise of criticism is tied, therefore, to Wilde's belief in the importance of self-development. The goal of life should be "not *doing* but *being*, and not *being* merely, but *becoming*." The ultimate work of art is what one makes of one's life. And criticism is vital to this process, for criticism sets us free. "Unlimited and absolute is the vision of him who sits at ease and watches."

Great criticism is as difficult to achieve as great art. And Wilde realized that "perhaps none of us can ever quite free ourselves from the influence of custom and the influence of novelty." Criticism, like art, is always

the product of a particular time and place; "any attempt to isolate it in any way from the progress and
movement and social life of the age that has produced
it would be to rob it of its true vitality, possibly to
mistake its true meaning." Wilde's own work is no
exception to this rule. In a longer study, it would be
useful to consider Wilde within the context of his age.
Original in many ways, he nevertheless drew heavily
upon the mainstream of nineteenth-century thought
even when he was rebelling against it. His often-
quoted observation that "nowadays people know the
price of everything and the value of nothing," is, for
example, but a distillation of what Ruskin had written
in *Unto This Last*. Indeed, in his early years, Wilde
was notorious for appropriating any idea that pleased
him. Laughing heartily at another's witticism, he once
declared, "I wish I'd said that!" To which James Whistler responded, "You will, Oscar, you will!"

Once close friends, Wilde and Whistler were no
longer on speaking terms by 1890. At mid-decade,
Wilde was imprisoned. And by 1900, he was dead. His
life illustrates the alienation from society that characterizes so many modern writers; in Wilde's case, this
alienation took the form of increasingly provocative
behavior until he found himself an exile, dying of
syphilis in a cheap Paris hotel. But Wilde's refusal to
conform to the social and sexual ethos of his age was
nonetheless responsible for much that is admirable in
his work.

In *A Woman of No Importance*, Lord Illingworth
remarks, "Moderation is a fatal thing . . . . Nothing
succeeds like excess." Wilde's career seems to be an
almost perfect illustration of this maxim. During the
early nineties, his behavior, both private and public,
became frankly self-indulgent. Yet his artistic development during these years was nothing less than remarkable. If *Lady Windermere's Fan* seems, at times,

to belong to the world of Victorian melodrama, *The Importance of Being Earnest* anticipates the world of Samuel Beckett.

As a playwright, Wilde was just coming into his own when, in 1895, he was sent to prison. There were to be no more comedies. The years in prison gave us *The Ballad of Reading Gaol*, the simplicity and power of which testify to a new stage in Wilde's development, a stage in which self-control triumphed over affectation. But the price for this poem was high, higher than its worth. It is a great and moving ballad. English literature, however, is rich in ballads, while there is nothing else quite like *The Importance of Being Earnest*.

It is futile to speculate on what further contributions Wilde might have made to the English theater. Having rediscovered the comedy of manners, he might have gone on to establish the theater of the absurd. For Wilde at his best was one of the most brilliant playwrights in English. He knew how to use language as few others have. Each generation since his death has brought forth some new exponent of the comedy of manners. We pass from Wilde to Maugham and on to Noel Coward, each imitation becoming weaker than the last until, in a Neil Simon, comedy degenerates into farce—the humor dependent upon whatever pleasure can be derived from watching Walter Matthau run about in his underwear. Seen in terms of his successors, Wilde was rare indeed.

But Wilde was more than a playwright—he was also a critic, a "true critic" in terms of his own criteria. A serious scholar, well-versed in Greek and Latin, fluent in French, and alive to beauty, Wilde knew how to select from "the cumbersome mass of creative work" achievement of enduring value. He helped us to rediscover Poe when Poe was remembered only as a drunk. He praised Yeats and Shaw, Ibsen and Dostoevsky, long before it became fashionable to do so. And his consistent plea for artistic autonomy is all too relevant today, when the impulse to censor beats fiercely in so many hearts.

As a writer, Wilde is uneven to say the least. But he continues to engage even when he falters. We have seen how *The Picture of Dorian Gray,* his only novel, suffers from a number of flaws. But it is a pleasure to read, however muddled its thesis. And the same might be said of his stories—contrived and sometimes long-winded, they continue to be read: a test for literary merit that cannot be easily dismissed.

Wilde once wrote of Byron that he wasted himself in battling with stupidity and hypocrisy: "Such battles do not always intensify strength: they often exaggerate weakness." As a result, he concluded, "Byron was never able to give us what he might have given us." If this is true of Byron, it is even truer of Wilde. To survey his career is to come ultimately to a horrible sense of waste—a major talent of minor accomplishment.

Notes

1. FEASTING WITH PANTHERS: THE RISE AND FALL OF OSCAR WILDE

1. George Bernard Shaw, "My Memories of Oscar Wilde," in *Oscar Wilde*, by Frank Harris (Michigan State University Press, 1959), p. 330.
2. H. Montgomery Hyde, *Oscar Wilde* (New York: Farrar, Straus and Giroux, 1975), p. 38.
3. Hesketh Pearson, *Oscar Wilde: His Life and Wit* (New York: Harper & Brothers, 1946), p. 39.
4. Reginald Bunthorne, the character in question, was probably modeled on Swinburne, who was much better known than Wilde. On the other hand, Bunthorne is "Such a judge of blue-and-white and other kinds of pottery / From early oriental down to modern terr-cotta-ry." Wilde often proclaimed his love of blue and white china, so the figure may be a composite.
5. "Impressions of America," in *The Artist as Critic: Critical Writings of Oscar Wilde*, ed. Richard Ellmann (New York: Random House, 1969), pp. 9–10.
6. Hyde, p. 77.
7. *The Letters of Oscar Wilde*, ed. Rupert Hart-Davis (New York: Harcourt Brace & World, 1962), p. 117.
8. Hyde, p. 89.
9. Hyde, p. 106.
10. *Letters*, pp. 195–196.
11. William Butler Yeats, as quoted in Hyde, p. 114.
12. Ross was seventeen at the time, and Wilde thirty-two.

Ross boasted that he seduced Wilde shortly after they first met. Richard Ellmann notes that in *The Picture of Dorian Gray*, Basil Hallward is murdered by Dorian Gray just before the latter turns thirty-eight. But the original text specified that Dorian was about to turn thirty-two, so the change is worth noting. "Wilde evidently considered this sudden alteration of his life a pivotal matter to be recast as Dorian's murder of Basil Hallward." Richard Ellmann, "The Critic as Artist as Wilde," in his *Wilde and the Nineties* (Princeton: Princeton University Library, 1966), p. 11.

13. George Bernard Shaw, as quoted by the Marquess of Queensberry, in *Oscar Wilde and the Black Douglas* (London: Hutchinson & Co., 1949), p. 25.

14. Harris, p. 105.

15. *Letters*, p. 326.

16. *Letters*, p. 426.

17. Erratic even in his spelling, Queensberry actually misspelled his famous charge, writing the key word as "somdomite".

18. Complete transcripts are available in *The Trials of Oscar Wilde*, ed. H. Montgomery Hyde (London: William Hodge & Co., 1949).

19. Hyde, *The Trials of Oscar Wilde*, p. 339.

20. Wilde was tried together with Alfred Taylor, who had been previously convicted of a similar offense. This in itself was prejudicial to Wilde's case. Hyde, *Oscar Wilde*, p. 228.

21. *Letters*, pp. 490–491.

2.   A MODERN GOTHIC: *The Picture of Dorian Gray*

1. Dorian's behavior in this scene is closely paralleled by the behavior of Mrs. Vane (Sibyl's mother) on the eve of her son's departure for Australia. When her son asks her if she was married to his father, "it reminded her of a bad rehearsal." But when the boy threatens to kill anyone who harms his sister, Mrs.

Vane comes suddenly alive: "The exaggerated folly of the threat, the passionate gesture that accompanied it, the mad melodramatic words, made life seem more vivid to her. She was familiar with the atmosphere . . . . She would have liked to have continued the scene on the same emotional scale, but he cut her short . . . . The moment was lost in vulgar details . . . . She was conscious that a great opportunity had been wasted." Like Dorian Gray, Mrs. Vane prefers acting to life.

2. *Letters*, p. 352.
3. Wilde repeats this line in *Lady Windermere's Fan*, Act III. Lord Darlington uses it to define a cynic.
4. In "About Oscar Wilde," in *Other Inquisitions*, trans. Ruth Simms (New York: Simon & Schuster, 1968), p. 81.
5. *Letters*, p. 258.
6. "The Decay of Lying," in *The Artist as Critic*, p. 299.
7. Ibid., p. 305.
8. Ibid., p. 301.
9. Ibid., p. 300.

3. COMMERCIAL SUCCESS: *Lady Windermere's Fan, A Woman of No Importance,* AND *An Ideal Husband*

1. Wilde had earlier used this line to describe Lady Narborough in *The Picture of Dorian Gray*.
2. Louis Kronenberger, "Oscar Wilde," in *The Thread of Laughter: English Stage Comedy from Jonson to Maugham* (New York: Hill & Wang, 1952), p. 213.
3. Quoted in Hyde, *Oscar Wilde*, p. 172.
4. See also "The Soul of Man Under Socialism": "In old days men had the rack. Now we have the press. That is an improvement certainly. But still it is very bad, and wrong, and demoralizing. Somebody—was it Burke?—called journalism the fourth estate . . . . But at the present moment it really is the only estate. It has eaten up the other three. The Lords Temporal say nothing, the Lords Spiritual have nothing to say, and the House of Commons has nothing to say and

says it. We are dominated by Journalism . . . . The
tyranny that it proposes to exercise over people's
private lives seems to me to be quite extraordinary"
(*The Artist as Critic*, p. 276).

5. E. H. Mikhail, "Self-Revelation in *An Ideal Husband*,"
    Modern Drama, 11 (September 1968), p. 183.
6. Arthur Ganz, "The Divided Self in the Society
    Comedies of Oscar Wilde," in *British Victorian Litera-
    ture*, ed. Shiv Kumar (New York: New York Univer-
    sity Press, 1969), pp. 489–490.
7. Morse Peckham, "What did Lady Windermere
    Learn?" *College English*, 18 (October 1956), p. 12.

4.   EXPLORING THE ABSURD: *The Importance of Being Earnest*

1. Mary McCarthy, "The Unimportance of Being
    Oscar," in *Sights and Spectacles: Theatre Chronicles
    1937–1956* (New York: Meridian, 1957), p. 108.
2. See also Lord Illingworth in *A Woman of No Im-
    portance*: "It is perfectly monstrous the way people
    go about, nowadays, saying things against one behind
    one's back that are absolutely and entirely true."
3. See also Lord Goring in *An Ideal Husband*: "Every-
    body one meets is a paradox nowadays. It is a great
    bore. It makes society so obvious."
4. Quoted in Harris, p. 332.
5. Quoted in Harris, p. 333.
6. Morris Freedman, "The Modern Tragicomedy of
    Wilde and O'Casey," in *The Moral Impulse* (Carbon-
    dale: Southern Illinois University Press, 1967), p. 63.
7. David Parker, "Oscar Wilde's Greatest Farce: *The
    Importance of Being Earnest*," *Modern Language
    Quarterly*, 35 (June 1974), p. 176.
8. See "The Critic as Artist": "Let me say to you now
    that to do nothing at all is the most difficult thing in
    the world, the most difficult and the most intellectual."
    The Artist as Critic, p. 381.

5. MANNERED MORALITY: *The Happy Prince* AND
          A House of Pomegranates

1. Pearson, pp. 120–121.
2. Quoted by Edouard Roditi, in *Oscar Wilde* (Norfolk, Conn.: New Directions, 1947), p. 71.
3. *Letters*, p. 302.

6. THE MAN OF SORROWS: *De Profundis* AND
          The Ballad of Reading Gaol

1. Douglas always denied that he had received the copy that Ross claimed to have sent him. H. Montgomery Hyde suggests that Douglas might have received the letter but destroyed it after reading the first few pages, convincing himself in later years that he had never seen it.
2. The implication that Douglas had abandoned Wilde is unfair. Despite the risk that he might have been arrested as well, Douglas remained in London during Wilde's trials, visiting Wilde regularly in Holloway Prison when his friend was detained without bail. He went abroad, at the request of his family, only after he had discussed this move with Wilde. And it should also be remembered that Wilde's correspondence was severely restricted while he was in prison.
3. Lord Alfred Douglas, *Oscar Wilde and Myself* (London: John Long, 1914), p. 84.
4. Cf. p. 17.
5. See also Dorian Gray, who wished "to be the spectator of one's own life."
6. Upon his release from prison, Wilde wrote a lengthy letter to the *Daily Chronicle* protesting the treatment of children in prison. After having described the disgusting quality of prison food, Wilde declared: "A child who has been crying all day long, and perhaps half the night, in a lonely dimly-lit cell, and is preyed upon by terror, simply cannot eat food of this coarse, horrible kind." A warder took pity upon one such child, "a tiny little chap, for whom they had

evidently been unable to find clothes small enough to fit." The warder gave the child a biscuit, and for this act of charity was instantly dismissed. (It is worth recording that one of Wilde's first acts upon leaving prison was to pay the fines of three such children—the only ones of whom he had knowledge—enabling them to go free.) In the same letter, Wilde protested against the treatment of the half-witted, describing in painful detail the story of a man who was beaten until he went mad (*Letters*, pp. 568–574).

7. THE DIALECTIC OF A DANDY: WHAT WILDE BELIEVED

1. Richard Ellmann made these available in *The Artist as Critic* (New York: Random House, 1969).

2. His idealism led him to conclude: "When there is no punishment at all, crime will either cease to exist, or if it occurs, will be treated by physicians as a very distressing form of dimentia, to be cured by care and kindness." He also believed: "Under Individualism people will be quite natural and absolutely unselfish . . . " In a similar vein, he once argued that art "by creating a common intellectual atmosphere between all countries, might . . . make men such brothers that they would not go out to slay one another for the whim or folly of some king or minister."

3. Matthew Arnold, "Preface to *Poems*" (1853), in *Poetry and Criticism of Matthew Arnold*, ed. A. Dwight Culler (Boston: Houghton Mifflin, 1961), p. 204.

4. Wilde cites, for example, "the silly boys who, after reading the adventures of Jack Sheppard or Dick Turpin, pillage the stalls of unfortunate apple-women, break into sweet-shops at night, and alarm old gentlemen who are returning home from the city by leaping out on them in suburban lanes, with black masks and unloaded revolvers."

Bibliography

Works by Oscar Wilde

Newdigate Prize Poem: Ravenna. Oxford: Thomas Shrimpton and Son, 1878. *Poems*. London: David Bogue, 1881.

The Happy Prince and Other Tales ("The Happy Prince," "The Nightingale and the Rose," "The Selfish Giant," "The Devoted Friend," "The Remarkable Rocket"). London: David Nutt, 1888.

Intentions ("The Decay of Lying," "Pen Pencil and Poison," "The Critic as Artist," "The Truth of Masks"). London: James Osgood, McIlvaine & Co., 1891.

The Picture of Dorian Gray. London: Ward, Lock, & Co., 1891.

Lord Arthur Savile's Crime and Other Stories ("Lord Arthur Savile's Crime," "The Sphinx Without a Secret," "The Canterville Ghost," "The Model Millionaire"). London: James Osgood, McIlvaine & Co., 1891.

A House of Pomegranates ("The Young King," "The Birthday of the Infanta," "The Fisherman and His Soul," "The Star Child"). London: James Osgood, McIlvaine & Co., 1891.

Salomé. Paris: Librairie de l'Art Indépendant, 1893.

Lady Windermere's Fan. London: Elkin Mathews and John Lane, 1893.

The Sphinx. London: Elkin Mathews and John Lane, 1894.

A Woman of No Importance. London: John Lane, 1894.

The Soul of Man. London: privately printed, 1895. (Reprinted from the *Fortnightly Review*, February 1891.)

The Ballad of Reading Gaol. London: Leonard Smithers 1898.

The Importance of Being Earnest. London: Leonard Smithers & Co., 1899.

An Ideal Husband. London: Leonard Smithers & Co., 1899.

De Profundis. London: Methuen & Co., 1905.

The Works of Oscar Wilde. London: Methuen & Co., 1908. Thirteen volumes.

The Letters of Oscar Wilde. Ed. Rupert Hart-Davis. New York: Harcourt Brace & World, 1962.

SELECTED BOOKS AND ARTICLES ON OSCAR WILDE

Bashford, Bruce. "Oscar Wilde: His Criticism and His Critics." *English Literature in Transition*, 20 (1977), 181–187.

———. "Oscar Wilde and Subjectivist Criticism." *English Literature in Transition*, 21 (1978), 218–234.

Borges, Jorge Luis. "About Oscar Wilde." In *Other Inquisitions*, trans. Ruth Simms. New York: Simon & Schuster, 1968.

Butwin, Joseph. "'The Martyr Clown: Oscar Wilde in *De Profundis*." *Victorian Newsletter*, 42 (Fall 1972), 1–6.

Douglas, Lord Alfred. *Oscar Wilde and Myself.* London: John Long, 1914.

Ellmann, Richard, et al. *Wilde and the Nineties.* Princeton: Princeton University Library, 1966.

Foster, Richard. "Wilde as Parodist." *College English*, 18 (October 1956), 18–23.

Freedman, Morris. "The Modern Tragicomedy of Wilde and O'Casey." In *The Moral Impulse.* Carbondale: Southern Illinois University Press, 1967.

Ganz, Arthur. "The Divided Self in the Society Comedies of Oscar Wilde." In *British Victorian Literature.* Ed. Shiv Kumar. New York: New York University Press, 1969.

Gide, Andre. *Oscar Wilde.* Ed. Stuart Mason. Oxford: The Holywell Press, 1905.

Gregor, Ian. "Comedy and Oscar Wilde." *Sewanee Review*, 74 (Spring 1966), 501–521.

Hardwick, Michael. *The Osprey Guide to Oscar Wilde*. London: Osprey, 1973.

Harris, Frank. *Oscar Wilde*, including "My Memories of Oscar Wilde" by George Bernard Shaw. 1916; rpt. East Lansing: Michigan State University Press, 1959.

Holland, Vyvyan. *Oscar Wilde*. London: Thames and Hudson, 1960.

Hyde, H. Montgomery. *Trials of Oscar Wilde*. London: William Hodge, 1949.

————. *Oscar Wilde*. New York: Farrar, Straus, and Giroux, 1975.

Jullian, Philippe. *Oscar Wilde*, trans. Violet Wyndham. London: Constable & Co., 1969.

Keefe, Robert. "Artist and Model in *The Picture of Dorian Gray*." *Studies in the Novel*, 5 (Spring 1973), 62–69.

Kronenberger, Louis. "Oscar Wilde." In *The Thread of Laughter: English Stage Comedy from Jonson to Maugham*. New York: Hill and Wang, 1952.

Lewis, Lloyd, and Henry Justin Smith. *Oscar Wilde Discovers America*. New York: Benjamin Bloom, 1967.

McCarthy, Mary. "The Unimportance of Being Oscar." In *Sights and Spectacles: Theatre Chronicles 1937–1956*. New York: Meridian, 1957.

Mason, Stuart. *Oscar Wilde: Art and Morality*. 1907; rpt. New York: Haskell House, 1971.

Mikhail, E. H. "Oscar Wilde and His First Comedy." *Modern Drama*, 10 (February 1968), 394–396.

————. "Self-Revelation in *An Ideal Husband*." *Modern Drama*, 11 (September 1968), 180–186.

Parker, David. "Oscar Wilde's Greatest Farce: *The Importance of Being Earnest*." *Modern Language Quarterly*, 35 (June 1974), 173–186.

Pearson, Hesketh. *Oscar Wilde: His Life and Wit*. New York: Harper & Brothers, 1946.

Peckham, Morse. "What Did Lady Windermere Learn?" *College English*, 18 (October 1956), 11–14.

Poague, L. A. "*The Importance of Being Earnest*: The

Texture of Wilde's Irony." *Modern Drama*, 16 (December 1973), 251–258.

Poteet, Lewis. *"Dorian Gray* and the Gothic Novel." *Modern Fiction Studies*, 17 (Summer 1971), 239–248.

Queensberry, Marquess of. *Oscar Wilde and the Black Douglas*. London: Hutchinson & Co., 1949.

Quintus, John Allen. "The Moral Prerogative in Oscar Wilde: A Look at the Fairy Tales." *Virginia Quarterly Review*, 53 (Autumn 1977), 708–717.

Reinert, Otto. "Satiric Strategy in *The Importance of Being Earnest*." *College English*, 18 (October 1956), 14–18.

Roditi, Edouard. *Oscar Wilde*. Norfolk, Conn.: New Directions, 1947.

Spininger, Dennis. "The Sense of the Absurd in *The Importance of Being Earnest*." *Papers on Language & Literature*, 12 (Winter 1976), 49–72.

Stavros, George. "Oscar Wilde and the Romantics." *English Literature in Transition*, 20 (1977), 35–45.

Stone, Geoffrey. "Serious Bunburyism: The Logic of *The Importance of Being Earnest*." *Essays in Criticism*, 26 (January 1976), 28–41.

Sullivan, Kevin. *Oscar Wilde*. New York: Columbia University Press, 1972.

Winwar, Frances. *Oscar Wilde and the Yellow Nineties*. New York: Harper & Brothers, 1941.

INDEX